GOOGLE DRIVE ESSENTIALS

A CURRICULUM OF WORD PROCESSING,
SPREADSHEETS, PRESENTATIONS, GRAPHICS
AND FORMS SKILLS FOR YOUTH AND BEGINNERS
USING GOOGLE DRIVE

George Somers

Updated for Google Drive 2.0 (2014)

© 2014
George Somers
GglDriveForKids@gmail.com
Somers Productions
Turlock, CA
http://googledriveforkids.com

The Google Drive™ online storage service, the Google Mail™ webmail service and other Google properties mentioned in this book are trademarked by Google Inc. George Somers is not affiliated with Google Inc., and does not represent the company. The use of screenshots herein is for educational purposes only and is considered acceptable under trademark usage guidelines.

Dedications:
This textbook is dedicated to my wife, Rebecca, my constant supporter and encourager. Thank you for being my anchor during this process. I love you!

I also dedicate it to my children, Ashley and Jordan. May you always love learning, reading and sharing what you learn with others. I look forward to seeing what you can accomplish in life with the tools and knowledge I never had.

Last, but not least, I dedicate this textbook to Judy Blackburn, Principal at Our Lady of Mercy School in Merced, CA. Thank you for supporting me in this project and for your help in advancing our technology program.

George Somers

Table of Contents

Preface 5
Getting Started 8
   First Document 10
WORD PROCESSING 13
   What is Word Processing? 14
   Lesson WP1: Let's Get Word Processing... 14
      Opportunity WP1: 19
   Lesson WP2 - Print Options 21
      Opportunity WP2: 24
   Lesson WP3 - Find/Replace and Spell Check 26
      Find and Replace 26
      Opportunity WP3: 31
   Lesson WP4 33
      Lesson WP4.1 - Ways to Select Text 33
      Lesson WP4.2 - Cut, Copy, & Paste and Drag and Drop Editing 35
      Opportunity WP4: 41
   Lesson WP5 - Working with Fonts 43
      Opportunity WP5: 46
   Lesson WP6 - Paragraph Indents 48
      Opportunity WP6: 51
   Lesson WP7 - Paragraph Line Spacing 53
      Opportunity WP7 56
   Lesson WP8 - Paragraph Justification 58
      Opportunity WP8 61
   Lesson WP9 - Tabs 63
      Opportunity WP9 66
   Lesson WP10 - Adding a Graphic Object 68
      Opportunity WP10 72
   Lesson WP11 - Page Settings 74
      Opportunity WP11 77
   Lesson WP12 - Tables 79
      Opportunity WP12 83
SPREADSHEETS 85
   Lesson SS1: Exploring a Spreadsheet 87
      Opportunity SS1 91
   Lesson SS2: Simple Formulas 93
      Opportunity SS2 97
   Lesson SS3: Copy Formulas, Insert Columns and Rows 99
      Opportunity SS3 104
   Lesson SS4: MAX, MIN AND AVERAGE FUNCTIONS 106
      Opportunity SS4 108
   Lesson SS5: Absolute References 110
      Opportunity SS5 113

- Lesson SS6: Formatting text and cells...115
  - Opportunity SS6..118
- Lesson SS7: Borders, Conditional Formatting, Hide Gridlines.............................120
  - Opportunity SS7..123
- Lesson SS8: Formulas using Dates..125
  - Opportunity SS8..129
- Lesson SS9: Data Sort...131
  - Opportunity SS9..133
- Lesson SS10: Create a Chart (Same Worksheet) 135
  - Opportunity SS10..139
- Lesson SS11: Create a Chart (On Its Own Worksheet) 140
  - Opportunity SS11..143
- Lesson SS12: Using a Form to Collect Data in a Spreadsheet............................144
  - Opportunity SS12..149

PRESENTATIONS...151
- What is a Google Slides? 152
- Lesson SL1: Red Ribbon Week Presentation..154
  - Opportunity SL1..156
- Lesson SL2: Spell Check, Duplicate, Reorder and Delete Slides........................158
  - Opportunity SL2..161
- Lesson SL3: Images, WordArt, Change Background..163
  - Opportunity SL3..167
- Lesson SL4: Transitions, Animations, and Viewing Slideshows..........................169
  - Opportunity SL4..173
- Lesson SL5: Tables..174
  - Opportunity SL5..177
- Lesson SL6: Speaker Notes...179
  - Opportunity SL6..184
- Lesson SL7: Buttons and Hyperlinks..185
  - Opportunity SL7..189

GRAPHICS..193
- Lesson GR1: Basic Shapes, Lines and Line Styles...194
  - Opportunity GR1...199
- Lesson GR2: Draw, Duplicate, Rotate and Manipulate Complex Graphic Objects...............200
  - Opportunity GR2...203
- Lesson GR3: Alignment..205
  - Opportunity GR3...208
- Lesson GR4: Stacking Order..209
  - Opportunity GR4...211

Preface

Purpose

The purpose of this textbook is to introduce young people to valuable word processing, spreadsheet, presentation, graphics and forms skills using Google Drive (formerly Google Docs). My goal here is to provide a curriculum, complete with assessments, aimed for grades five through eight. However, **anyone** new to Google Drive and Google Apps will benefit from the skills taught in this textbook. I have searched the internet and asked my personal learning network for such a curriculum created by others in my situation, and have come up empty. So, I decided to draw upon my twenty plus years of teaching experience and write my own textbook.

In writing this book, it is NOT my intention to provide an exhaustive guide to Google Drive and Google Apps. I have simply desired to create the necessary materials necessary to meet the curricular needs of my students. As such, I want to thank the students of Our Lady of Mercy School for their evaluation of this book and its materials. I hope you find these materials to be valuable in your effective use the word processing, spreadsheet, presentation, graphics and forms applications provided by Google.

What are Google Drive and Google Apps?

Google Drive is Google's online service for storing and managing your documents in the "cloud". It is included with every as part of the services provided with every free Google account. Google Drive also includes Google Apps, which are online office productivity applications. Many of these applications can also be used offline. The core Google Apps are:
- Google Docs (word processing)
- Google Sheets (spreadsheets)
- Google Slides (presentations)
- Google Drawings
- Google Forms

Why Google Drive?

Limited school technology budgets often create an imbalance in the level of technology we can provide our students. Computer labs, classrooms and library media centers are often riddled with 10 year-old equipment sitting alongside 2 year-old equipment. New software won't run on the older machines and the new machines often can't run the aging software in which schools have invested their precious resources. Lessons frequently need to be designed to meet the lowest common denominator school technology budgets can provide. Add in computers which are no longer supported and updated by Microsoft and Apple, along with the lack of manpower to keep them running and you have a technological nightmare. Teaching students the essential skills they need to be successful learners and effective communicators in this environment is challenging, to say the least, using the substandard tools provided.

Enter Google Apps for Education. Google Apps, included with Google Drive, is FREE if you use less than 5GB of space![1] Being free, you would think Google Drive's offerings would be rough around the edges and lacking in essential features. There, you would be incorrect. I have found that Google Drive is a platform which provides a means for students to learn and practice the essential application skills they need to succeed. Google Drive surpasses the technology needs for my target student group - grades five through eight. I hope educators will find this curriculum useful in the education of their students.

Another advantage of Google Drive is that all student work is saved frequently online. Students can edit documents from any computer with an internet connection, including some mobile devices. There are no USB thumb drives to manage or threat of malware infections to keep a teacher awake at night. Google even manages the servers. What's not to love?

A Note about Google Gmail Accounts

While Google Apps for Education does include email accounts, email access is one of the Google Apps services which can be disabled, leaving the other Google Drive features unaffected. For more information about administering Google Apps for Education, please visit the Google Apps for Education website at http://www.google.com/apps/intl/en/edu. In addition, Google Drive is also available as part of Google Apps for Business and standard Google accounts.

Google Drive Software

Google Drive also includes a desktop client which copies the files in your online Google Drive and synchronizes them with a folder on your computer. This book will not cover this software. For more information about Google Drive software, visit https://drive.google.com.

Using this Book

The basic structure of this book is a sequential series of lessons which present a guided practice approach to the essential word processing, spreadsheet, graphics and presentation skills. The lessons in this book will prepare students and beginners for the corresponding assessment at the end of each lesson. I call them "Opportunities" because they give the students the chance to demonstrate the skills they learned in the lesson. These Opportunities are found at the end of each lesson.

---

[1] Additional Google Drive space can be purchased. Visit https://drive.google.com/ for pricing information.

About the Author

George Somers has been a technology educator in Central California since 1993. He currently teaches Kindergarten through eighth grades at Our Lady of Mercy School in Merced, CA. He is also an Adjunct Professor teaching Computer Applications for Merced College in Merced, CA. He is husband to his music teacher wife, Rebecca and father to a daughter and a son, Ashley and Jordan. For more information and to connect with George on the popular social networks, visit http://about.me/georgesomers. This book employs the lessons and assignments he has used in his teaching career.

Assumptions

The activities and projects contained in this book assume that you have either a Google Drive account (with no Google Gmail account) or a Google Gmail account (which includes Google Drive). Either a personal account, a Google Apps for Education, or a Google Apps for Business account will suffice. If your organization has a Google Apps account, see your system or network administrator to get an account. If you don't, go to http://google.com to get your own personal account. The use of Google e-mail accounts is not required to complete the exercises in the book.

Passwords

Regardless of whether your password is assigned or self-created, remember to keep it safe and do not share it with anyone. To avoid having your account compromised by a hacker, make your password strong by using the following guidelines:
- At least 8 character in length
- Don't use a word found in the dictionary
- Use numbers, a combination of upper and lowercase letters, and special characters such as &, % and $

A Note about Browsers

While Google Drive and Google Apps will work in all browsers, it has been my experience that Google Drive and Google Apps perform best in the Google Chrome browser. It is for this reason that all illustrations in the textbook are showing Google Drive as seen by Google Chrome, the recommended browser. In addition, some features, such as printing, work differently in non-Chrome browsers. Since I prefer the Chrome method, I use Chrome through this book. You can download Chrome for free from http://google.com/chrome.

Getting Started

This activity will get you acquainted with the basics of Google Drive (formerly Google Docs).

1. Launch an internet browser and go to http://drive.google.com and login (see left). Be

   sure to leave the "Stay signed in" box unchecked when at school or at a public computer.

2. If you have never signed in to this account before you may be presented with a privacy policy screen. To accept the privacy policy, click the **OK, got it** button.

2. You may also be presented with an introductory video (see below). If your teacher indicates to do so, go ahead and watch it

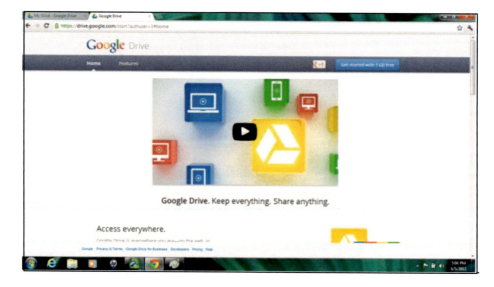

3. Next, create a folder for the documents you will create for this class. Here's how:
    a. On the left side of the webpage, click on the **NEW** button and choose **Folder** from the drop-down menu (see figure at bottom left).
    b. Optional: You may wish create a folder using your class name as specified by your teacher. For example, <class code> <assignment name> <full name>. Replace the bracketed labels with your information (example **Computers 8K**). Ask your teacher what to enter as the folder name (see figure bottom right).
    c. Your teacher may ask you to share your class folder with him/her by entering their email address. If so, ask your teacher for instructions on how to do this.

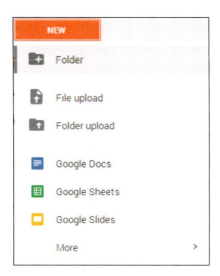
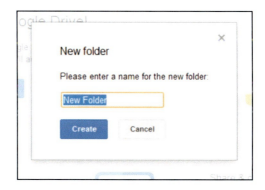

First Document

1. Create a new document by clicking the **NEW** button in the left navigation pane and choose **Google Docs**.

2. A new window or tab opens with your new document. It will look like the following figure.

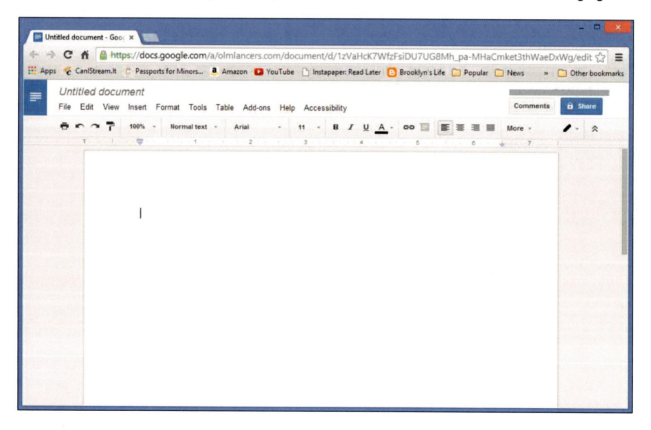

3. If you are required to use a specific assignment header at the top of your paper, type it in now at the top of your document.
4. Choose one of the following writing prompts and type a 50-100 word response:[2] Use your topic as your title.
    a. What I Did Over Summer Break
    b. Something Interesting I Learned In The Last Week
    c. My Favorite Musical Artist or Group
5. **Note:** As you type your document, **DO NOT** press the **ENTER** key (**RETURN** on Macs) until the end of a paragraph or to start a new paragraph. Google Drive will start a new line automatically. This is called **WORD WRAP** or **TEXT WRAP.**
6. **Note 2:** The new rule for ending sentences is one space (not two spaces) after a period, question mark or exclamation point.
7. Proofread your document and fix any errors.
    a. The **Insertion Point** is the blinking vertical line indicating where your typing is inserted as you type.
    b. The Insertion Point can be moved by either using the arrow keys on the keyboard or by clicking the **I-beam mouse pointer** (see right) in the document to move the insertion point to that location. Try both methods as you edit your document to fix any spelling or grammar errors.

    I-beam pointer

    c. Move the insertion point to the right of any edits you need to make.
    d. Press the **backspace key** (delete key on Macs) to erase each letter you need to remove.
    e. Type in the correct letters to correct your mistake.
    f. Read it one more time before considering your document finished.

---

[2] Hint: You can get your word count by going to Google Drive's **Tools** menu and selecting **Word Count**.

8. Save the document with a new name. Here's how:

    a. Go to Google Drive's **File** menu and choose **Rename...**

    b. Save with "8K <Assignment name> <student full name>" or use your teacher's preferred naming system.

    c. Click the **OK** button.

9. Optional: Add the teacher as a collaborator on this document. To do this...

    a. Click on the **Share** button in the upper right corner of the webpage.

    b. In the sharing box that comes up (see figure at right), enter your teacher's email address in the **Add People** field.

    c. Make sure your teacher has **edit** privileges and click the **DONE** button (see bottom right).[3]

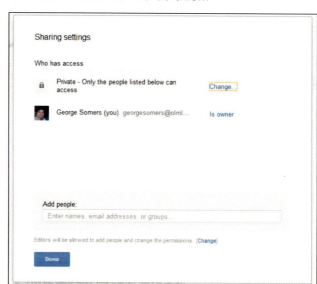

10. Print the document <u>if your teacher says to do so</u> by choosing **Print** from Google Drive's **File** menu. Click the **Print** button on the next screen.

    a. Close the document's tab by clicking the **x** on the right end of the tab.

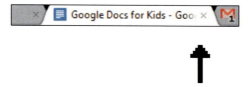

---

[3] Shared documents will show up in the recipient's **Incoming** area which is located in the left side navigation bar in Google Drive.

WORD PROCESSING

GOOGLE DOCS

What is Word Processing?

Word Processing is the process of using an application, such as Microsoft Word or Google Drive, to enter text, save, edit, and print (or share electronically) text-based files. The files that you create with these applications are called **documents**. The applications (or software) that you use to create your documents are called **word processors**. Learning word processing skills will allow you to effectively communicate using text-based documents on the computer. In this book, you will learn basic word processing skills which are features of any word processor.

One of the advantages to using Google Drive is that it saves your work extremely frequently so you will never have to worry about saving your changes.

Lesson WP1: Let's Get Word Processing...

In this lesson, we'll learn about the ruler bar, editing text, selecting text, renaming a document and printing a document. We will also practice saving a document and sharing a document. If you need to review these concepts, please see "Chapter 1: Getting Started".

The **ruler** across the top of your window shows you the horizontal width of the page, with the exception of the left and right margin. The ruler marks the area of the page in which you can type. Using the figure below, find the ruler in your window.

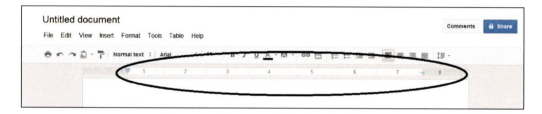

How big are your left and right margins (outside the boundaries of the ruler)?

Now, you will type your first document for the word processing unit. We will use this document as the base document for several lessons in this book, so do your best work. At the end of the lesson, your document will look like what you see on the next page. For instructions, turn to page 16.

Dear Preferred Customer;

Today, we are introducing a technology product that will blow your mind. The new Butler Pad from Enhanced Home Technologies will serve all your home automation needs. From turning on your lights to setting your lawn sprinkler system, the Butler Pad is literally at your command. Simply use your voice to control all aspects of your Butler Pad system. It's your personal butler!

Today, Bart Stone has built Enhanced Home Technologies into an international home technology leader. With over 100 life-changing products and over 1250 patents, Enhanced Home Technologies has more than 20 offices worldwide. Its products are found in 5-star hotels and mansions of the rich and famous. Now, we are taking advantage of more efficient manufacturing processes to make this technology affordable for every family.

Enhanced Home Technologies is no stranger to innovation. From its founding in 1997 by technology visionary Bart Stone, Enhanced Home Technologies has been a leader in household electronics. That same year, he launched his first home product, the digital picture frame. In 2000, we introduced the world's first internet-connected thermostat. That product was followed by the first Internet-connected refrigerator and microwave in 2005.

We invite you to come see a demonstration at a local home improvement store near you. Once you see this home automation system in action, you will never know how you lived without it. Not only is it convenient, but it will learn your living habits and save you money on your electrical bill in the process.

You can visit our website, http://enhanced-home-technologies.com for video demonstrations of our line of products. You can also find product, pricing, and contact information there.

Sincerely,

<Student Name>
Residential Technologies Unit

P.S. Order in the next two weeks and you'll get a free consultation and save 15% on a Butler Pad system. Don't miss out on this great opportunity. You'll be saving money now to lower your energy bills later.

INSTRUCTIONS:

1. Create a new Google Doc (New > Google Docs).
2. Name it "Butler Pad" (File > Rename)
3. Type the first paragraph as shown below. Do not indent. Be sure to include the semicolon (;) at the end.

   Dear Preferred Customer;

4. Press the **ENTER** key (**RETURN** on Mac Computers) <u>TWO TIMES</u> -- once to end the paragraph, and a second time to skip a line.

5. Now type the second paragraph as shown below. Remember, do not hit the **ENTER (RETURN)** key until you are at the end of the paragraph. Notice that Google Drive will automatically start a new line in your paragraph as needed. This feature is called **Word Wrap** and is common among all word processors. For this lesson, we'll be skipping a line between the body (main section) of our letter. **Note:** your lines may differ from those shown below, but each paragraph will match the paragraphs on page 15.

   Today, we are introducing a technology product that will blow your mind. The new Butler Pad from Enhanced Home Technologies will serve all your home automation needs. From turning on your lights to setting your lawn sprinkler system, the Butler Pad is literally at your command. Simply use your voice to control all aspects of your Butler Pad system. It's your personal butler!

6. Great! Now press the **ENTER (RETURN)** key twice and type the remaining body paragraphs as follows. Remember to skip a line between paragraphs and put only one space after a sentence.

   Today, Bart Stone has built Enhanced Home Technologies into an international home technology leader. With over 100 life-changing products and over 1250 patents, Enhanced Home Technologies has more than 20 offices worldwide. Its products are found in 5-star hotels and mansions of the rich and famous. Now, we are taking advantage of more efficient manufacturing processes to make this technology affordable for every family.

   Enhanced Home Technologies is no stranger to innovation. From its founding in 1997 by technology visionary Bart Stone, Enhanced Home Technologies has been a leader in household electronics. That same year, he launched his first home product, the digital picture frame. In 2000, we introduced the world's first internet-connected thermostat. That product was followed by the first Internet-connected refrigerator and microwave in 2005.

   We invite you to come see a demonstration at a local home improvement store near you. Once you see this home automation system in action, you will never know how you lived without it. Not only is it convenient, but it will learn your living habits and save you money on your electrical bill in the process.

You can visit our website, http://enhanced-home-technologies.com for video demonstrations of our line of products. You can also find product, pricing, and contact information there.

Whew! That was a lot of typing. You may have noticed that, after typing the web address in the last paragraph, the address becomes blue and underlined. It is now a **hyperlink**. A hyperlink is an active link that will take you to a specific website when you click it.

7. We're almost done now. For our signature line, we'll need to skip an extra line. So, press **ENTER (RETURN)** three times and type:

    Sincerely,

8. Now press **ENTER(RETURN)** four times and type your full name (first and last).

9. Press **ENTER (RETURN)** again type:

    Residential Technologies Division

We'll leave the P.S. off the letter for now. First we need to proofread the letter. As we did in the *Getting Started* chapter, move your insertion point using the mouse or the arrow keys, delete the incorrect letters and type in the correct letters as needed. Also, if you see words that are underlined with red dots (see below), you can right-click on the words and replace them with a suggestion from the pop-up menu if it is listed there.

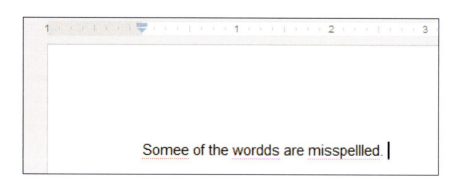

Nice job! Now, we want to add the P.S. on the end of our letter but we want to keep this version too. To do that, we'll need to save this document with a different name so we can make changes.

Here's how to make a **copy** and **rename** our new document:

1. Go to Google Drive's **File** and menu and choose **Make a copy...**
2. In the box that appears, enter the new name **Promotion** and click the **OK** button (see figure at right).
3. Later, we'll move this document into your folder for this class.

Now let's add our P.S. paragraph. Make sure your insertion point is still at the end of the document. If it isn't, move your insertion point to the end of the last line and press the **ENTER (RETURN)** key twice.

Now type the P.S. paragraph as shown:

> **P.S. Order in the next two weeks and you'll get a free consultation and save 15% on a new Butler Pad system. Don't miss out on this great opportunity. You'll be saving money now to lower your energy bills later.**

You now have two similar documents -- the original **Butler Pad** and the new **Promotion** with the P.S. paragraph. Want proof? Let me show you.

Close the **Promotion** and **Butler Pad** tabs and you should be back at the Google Drive page. If you are not there, click the tab named **"My Drive - Google Drive"** in your browser.

On your Google Drive page, you will see both the **Promotion** and **Butler Pad** documents. Click on the **Butler Pad** document and notice that you do not have the P.S. paragraph. Close this tab and return to the Google Drive page.

Similarly, open the **Promotion** document and notice that you DO have the P.S. paragraph in that document. If so, you have successfully completed this lesson.

Now, close your browser. In the Google Drive window, drag the **Butler Pad** and **Promotions** file onto your folder for this class. This will move those files into that folder so they are organized.

You are now ready to proceed to the **WP1 Opportunity**. We call them "opportunities" because you will have the opportunity to show what you have learned in this lesson.

Opportunity WP1:

Follow the steps below to produce the document as displayed on the next page. The purpose of this assignment is to give you the opportunity to show what you learned from the lesson. If allowed by your teacher, you can refer to the lesson pages to refresh your memory.

1. Log into Google Drive and create a new document.
2. **Name** the document **Opportunity WP1** or a variation as directed by your teacher.
3. Type your assignment header (name, assignment, date, subject, etc.) as directed by your teacher.
4. Type the text as shown on the next page. Skip a line between each paragraph. Remember, only press the enter (return) key at the end of a paragraph or to skip a line.
5. Proofread your document to check for spelling and grammar errors.
6. If your teacher wants you to print this document, do so now.
7. Close the tab for this document.
8. Move the document to your class folder.
9. If you are to turn this document in electronically, follow your teacher's directions for submitting your document.
10. Close the document's tab and move it to your class folder.

E-books Supercharge Reading

E-books, or electronic books, are becoming more and more popular these days. E-book reader devices like the Nook from Barnes and Noble and Amazon's line of Kindle products are becoming increasingly common. These devices have many features students and consumers have found very useful.

First, the 2012 models can hold anywhere from 1,000 and 3,500 books, all at your fingertips. They are lightweight, weighing as little as 6 ounces. E-books can be purchased inexpensively; however e-textbooks remain priced comparably with their expensive printed versions. These e-books can be purchased wirelessly and appear on the device seconds after the purchase is complete. They come in varying sizes as well, with some products offering displays as small as 6 inches or as big as 10 inches. Most of these devices can go weeks without a battery recharge.

In addition to their portability, e-book readers have many features to help those with special needs. Text sizes can be increased at will to help visually challenged readers. Some e-readers support audible reading of the text to help those with sight issues.

Some e-book readers are now providing other features, such as calendar and mail applications and the ability to play games purchased electronically and cheaply. Apple's iPad was the first to offer such features. The iPad, a tablet with e-reader functionality, was announced in 2010 and has remained dominant in the tablet market ever since. Other manufacturers offer less expensive options but with fewer features and/or decreased performance when compared to the iPad.

These e-readers have made the activity of reading more mobile and convenient. While retail bookstore chains are challenged to keep their doors open, e-readers are bringing the store to consumers. Lawrence Clark Powell once said:

"We are the children of a technological age. We have found streamlined ways of doing much of our routine work. Printing is no longer the only way of reproducing books. Reading them, however, has not changed."

It won't be long before heavy school textbooks are replaced with e-readers holding all the information they could ever need in one small device.

Lesson WP2 - Print Options

Printing is one form of outputting your document on paper using a printer. This is also called a **hardcopy**. In this lesson, we will learn about the Google Drive's printing options. You may or may not be printing this lesson. Ask your teacher if he/she wants you to print it. Regardless, you should complete this lesson to learn about the printing options available to you. At the end of this lesson, you can either print the lesson or cancel it.

To begin this lesson, log in to Google Drive and open your **Promotion** document by clicking on it.

Go to Google Drive's **File** menu and choose **Print**. The print window opens and looks like this...

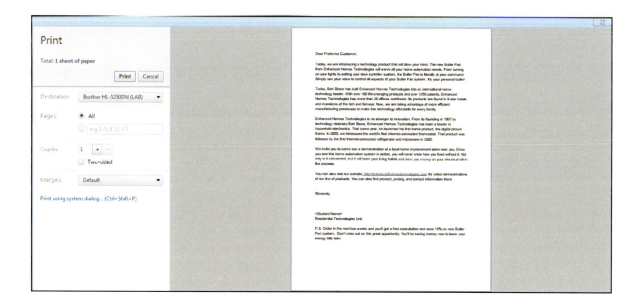

Your options are on the left side and your preview is on the right. The default (or normal) settings are to print one copy to your regular printer. But you may need to use other settings. We will learn about these options in this lesson.

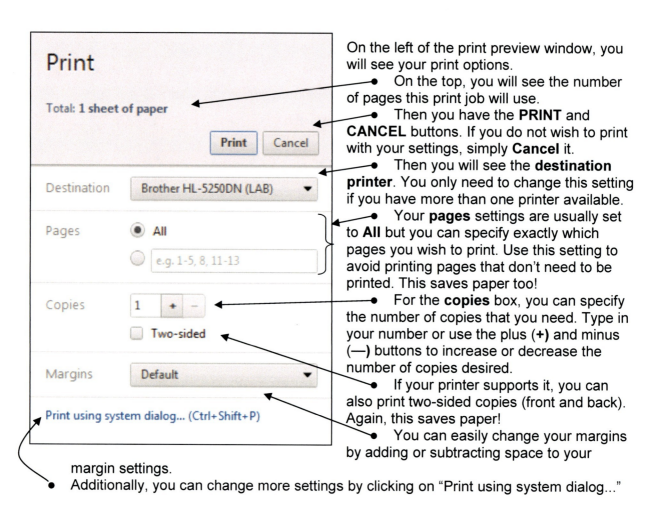

On the left of the print preview window, you will see your print options.
- On the top, you will see the number of pages this print job will use.
- Then you have the **PRINT** and **CANCEL** buttons. If you do not wish to print with your settings, simply **Cancel** it.
- Then you will see the **destination printer**. You only need to change this setting if you have more than one printer available.
- Your **pages** settings are usually set to **All** but you can specify exactly which pages you wish to print. Use this setting to avoid printing pages that don't need to be printed. This saves paper too!
- For the **copies** box, you can specify the number of copies that you need. Type in your number or use the plus (**+**) and minus (**—**) buttons to increase or decrease the number of copies desired.
- If your printer supports it, you can also print two-sided copies (front and back). Again, this saves paper!
- You can easily change your margins by adding or subtracting space to your margin settings.
- Additionally, you can change more settings by clicking on "Print using system dialog..."

First, make whatever changes you want to these settings but do not print. You will see these changes reflected in your preview. Experiment with the settings for a few minutes, then click the **Cancel** button.

There's one more print setting we need to learn. Regular print jobs will print in **Portrait** orientation (or vertical). You can also print in horizontal or **Landscape** mode. This orientation is great for signs and other documents which need to be wide instead of tall.

You can change paper orientation, page size, margins and other options in the **Page Setup** box. We'll discuss margins in another lesson.

To bring up the **Print Setup** box, go to Google Drive's **File** menu and choose **Page Setup**. Change the orientation to **Landscape** and click the **OK** button.

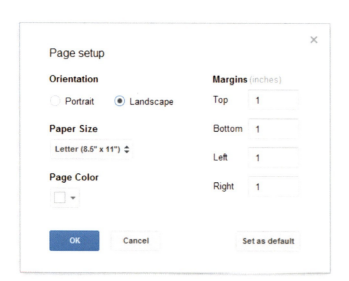
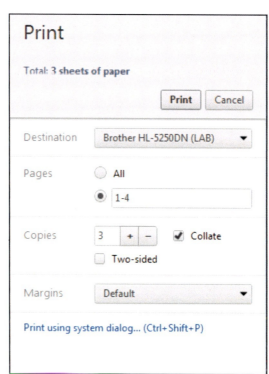

Now go to the **File** menu and choose **Print**. Change your settings to match the settings above (on the right).

Unless your teacher tells you to print your document, after entering these settings, click **Cancel**.

Close your document and move it to your class folder in Google Drive.

Great job! You are now ready for the **WP2 Opportunity**.

A Note about Printing and Browsers:

Although you can print from Google Drive in any current browser (e.g. Chrome, Firefox, Safari, Internet Explorer), printing using the Google Chrome browser is easier. Here's why.

When you print from Google Drive with a browser that is not Google Chrome, Google Drive creates a PDF document. A **PDF** file is a picture of your printed page. To print this file you will need to open it in Adobe Reader (Windows), Preview (Mac) or similar PDF reader software. Once the file is open, print it by choosing the usual method, such as **File > Print**.

Google Chrome, on the other hand, will send your document directly to the printer. No second PDF step is necessary. For this reason, I recommend using Google Chrome whenever you are working in Google Drive. Since it is a free download (http://google.com/chrome), go ahead and install it (kids, ask your parents) so you can use Google Drive at home.

Opportunity WP2:

Print Options

Follow the steps below to produce the document as displayed on the next page. The purpose of this assignment is to give you the opportunity to show what you learned from the lesson. If allowed by your teacher, you can refer to the lesson pages to refresh your memory.

1. Log into Google Drive and **open Opportunity WP1** from your class folder.
2. **Make a copy** and name the document **Opportunity WP2** or a variation as directed by your teacher.
3. Type or edit your assignment header (name, assignment, date, subject, etc.) as directed by your teacher.
4. In Page setup, make the page orientation **Landscape.**
5. Use the Print command to print 2 copies of your document.
6. Staple the pages together and turn them in to your teacher.
7. Close the document's tab and move it to your class folder.

E-books Supercharge Reading

E-books, or electronic books, are becoming more and more popular these days. E-book reader devices like the Nook from Barnes and Noble and Amazon's line of Kindle products are becoming increasingly common. These devices have many features students and consumers have found very useful.

First, the 2012 models can hold anywhere from 1,000 and 3,500 books, all at your fingertips. They are lightweight, weighing as little as 6 ounces. E-books can be purchased inexpensively; however e-textbooks remain priced comparably with their expensive printed versions. These e-books can be purchased wirelessly and appear on the device seconds after the purchase is complete. They come in varying sizes as well, with some products offering displays as small as 6 inches or as big as 10 inches. Most of these devices can go weeks without a battery recharge.

In addition to their portability, e-book readers have many features to help those with special needs. Text sizes can be increased at will to help visually challenged readers. Some e-readers support audible reading of the text to help those with sight issues.

Some e-book readers are now providing other features, such as calendar and mail applications and the ability to play games purchased electronically and cheaply. Apple's iPad was the first to offer such features. The iPad, a tablet with e-reader functionality, was announced in 2010 and has remained dominant in the tablet market ever since. Other manufacturers offer less expensive options but with fewer features and/or decreased performance when compared to the iPad.

These e-readers have made the activity of reading more mobile and convenient. While retail bookstore chains are challenged to keep their doors open, e-readers are bringing the store to consumers. Lawrence Clark Powell once said;

"We are the children of a technological age. We have found streamlined ways of doing much of our routine work. Printing is no longer the only way of reproducing books. Reading them, however, has not changed."

It won't be long before heavy school textbooks are replaced with e-readers holding all the information they could ever need in one small device.

E-books Supercharge Reading

E-books, or electronic books, are becoming more and more popular these days. E-book reader devices like the Nook from Barnes and Noble and Amazon's line of Kindle products are becoming increasingly common. These devices have many features students and consumers have found very useful.

First, the 2012 models can hold anywhere from 1,000 and 3,500 books, all at your fingertips. They are lightweight, weighing as little as 6 ounces. E-books can be purchased inexpensively; however e-textbooks remain priced comparably with their expensive printed versions. These e-books can be purchased wirelessly and appear on the device seconds after the purchase is complete. They come in varying sizes as well, with some products offering displays as small as 6 inches or as big as 10 inches. Most of these devices can go weeks without a battery recharge.

In addition to their portability, e-book readers have many features to help those with special needs. Text sizes can be increased at will to help visually challenged readers. Some e-readers support audible reading of the text to help those with sight issues.

Some e-book readers are now providing other features, such as calendar and mail applications and the ability to play games purchased electronically and cheaply. Apple's iPad was the first to offer such features. The iPad, a tablet with e-reader functionality, was announced in 2010 and has remained dominant in the tablet market ever since. Other manufacturers offer less expensive options but with fewer features and/or decreased performance when compared to the iPad.

These e-readers have made the activity of reading more mobile and convenient. While retail bookstore chains are challenged to keep their doors open, e-readers are bringing the store to consumers. Lawrence Clark Powell once said;

"We are the children of a technological age. We have found streamlined ways of doing much of our routine work. Printing is no longer the only way of reproducing books. Reading them, however, has not changed."

It won't be long before heavy school textbooks are replaced with e-readers holding all the information they could ever need in one small device.

Lesson WP3 - Find/Replace and Spell Check

In this lesson, we'll learn about the **Find/Replace** and **Spell Check** tools.

Find and Replace

The **Find and Replace** tool will allow you to find words in your document. Using replace, you can change one word to another. This can be helpful if you consistently misspell words and want a fast way to change them. The Find and Replace box looks like the following:

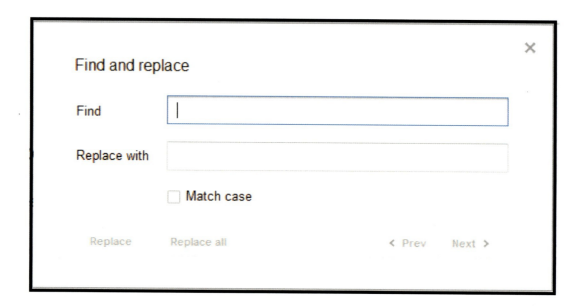

Optionally, the **Match case** check box can be used to find and replace only words that match the case as you specify. We will walk you through these and other options in this lesson.

Ready? Let's go! First, let's open the **Promotion** document from your Google Drive.

Make a copy (File menu) of this file and **rename** (File menu) it **Promotion WP3**. We covered these commands in Lesson WP1.

Let's try these **Find** searches
1. Bring up the Find and Replace box by going to the Google Drive's **Edit** menu and choosing **Find and Replace...**
2. In the Find box (or field), enter **home** and click the **Next** button. How many instances of this word are there in this document?
3. Now check the **Match case** box and click the **Next** button. How many instances of this word are found that are only lower case?

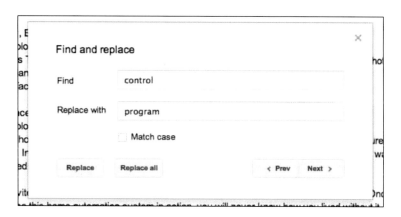

Now, let's try some **Find and Replace** searches.
4. Use Find and Replace to replace the word "control" with "program".
    a. Bring up the Find and Replace box by going to the Google Drive's **Edit** menu and choosing **Find and Replace...**
    b. Enter the find and replace words as shown in the figure above.
    c. Click the **Next** button.
    d. The box covers your document, however. To move the box to the side, click on the words "Find and replace" at the top and drag to the right or left. You will now see the instance of the word "control" highlighted.
    e. Click the **Replace** button.
    f. Close the Find and replace box by clicking the "**x**" in the upper right corner.
5. We will now replace all instances of "Enhanced Home Technologies". except the first one, with "EHT". Here's how.
    a. Open the find and replace box and enter the following using capitals as listed:
        i. **Find**: Enhanced Home Technologies
        ii. **Replace with:** EHT
    b. Check the **Match Case** box
    c. If the **Find and replace** box is covering your document, drag it out of the way.
    d. Click the **Next** button to see all instances of "Enhanced Home Technologies" in your document. The active one will be highlighted darker than the rest and you will see a count (like "2 of 5") on the right side of the **Find** field.
    e. For the first instance, click the **Next** button again to make no change.
    f. For all the other instances, click the **Replace** button to replace the company name with the acronym "EHT".
    g. **Close** the Find and replace box when you are done.

Spell Checking

Google Drive is constantly checking your spelling as you type. This feature is called **Spell Check**. It checks each word against its own dictionary of words. If it can't find the word, Google Drive will mark it by underlining it with red dots. However, Google Drive cannot tell you if you are using the CORRECT word. To prove this point, read the poem below.

A Little Poem Regarding Computer Spell Checkers...

**Eye halve a spelling chequer
It came with my pea sea
It plainly marques four my revue
Miss steaks eye kin knot sea.**

**Eye strike a key and type a word
And weight four it two say
Weather eye am wrong oar write
It shows me strait a weigh.**

**As soon as a mist ache is maid
It nose bee fore two long
And eye can put the error rite
Its rare lea ever wrong.**

**Eye have run this poem threw it
I am shore your pleased two no
Its letter perfect awl the weigh
My chequer tolled me sew.**

Anonymous

Every word in this poem is a valid word found in any dictionary. You will find that many of these words, however, are not the correct word in context. For example, words like "I" and "eye" sound correct when you read them, but the words mean something different. Spell check won't fix that. You must depend on your brain for that!

Correcting Flagged Words

One way to correct a flagged word is to right-click the word (CONTROL-click on some Mac's) and choose either the correct spelling from a list of suggestions, ignore the word or add it to your custom dictionary.

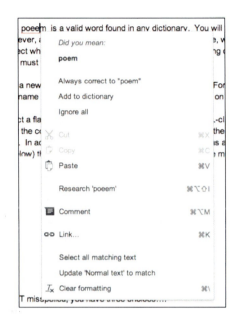

In addition to this menu option, Google Drive also has a Spell Check dialog box (see figure below) that will search your entire document for possible misspelled words.

If the word is NOT misspelled, you have three choices….

- **IGNORE**: If the word is correct, but you want to ignore it this time only, click the **Ignore** button.
- **IGNORE ALL** or **Add to Dictionary**: By pressing the down-arrow on the Ignore button, you get the option to **Ignore all** occurrences of the word in the document or **Add it to your dictionary**.

You can also add a new word to the dictionary if you know it is correct. For example, you may find that your last name is not in Google's dictionary. We will add it on the next page.

To practice with spell checking, let's purposely spell some words in **Promotion WP3** incorrectly. Then, we will fix them.

1. If you do not have the document **Promotion WP3** open, open it from your Google Drive window.
2. Create spelling errors in your document.
    a. Change the word *introducing* to **introduccing** in the first paragraph.
    b. Change the word *international* to **internationale** in the second paragraph.
    c. Change the word *technology* to **technlogy** in the second paragraph.
3. All three of these misspelled words are now underlined with red dots.
4. Correct your spelling errors.
    a. Right-click (shift-click on Mac) on the first incorrect word, *introduccing*.
    b. At the top of the pop-up menu that appears, under the words "Did you mean", you will find the correct spelling of the word.
    c. Click the correct spelling -- **introducing** -- and the word will be changed.
    d. Repeat this process to correct **internationale** and **technlogy.**
5. If your first and/or last name is flagged as being spelled incorrectly, add it to the dictionary by right-clicking (shift-clicking on Mac) and "Add to Dictionary". [4]

Close **Promotion WP3** and move it to your class folder in Google Drive.

You are now ready for **Opportunity WP3**.

---

[4] You can also choose "Ignore all" and Google Drive will simply ignore your name without adding it to the dictionary or flagging it as a spelling error.

Opportunity WP3:

Find/Replace and Spell Check

Follow the steps below to produce the document as displayed on the next page. The purpose of this assignment is to give you the opportunity to show what you learned from the lesson. If allowed by your teacher, you can refer to the lesson pages to refresh your memory.

1. Log into Google Drive and **open Opportunity WP1** from your class folder.
2. **Make a copy** and name the document **Opportunity WP3** or a variation as directed by your teacher.
3. Type or edit your assignment header (name, assignment, date, subject, etc.) as directed by your teacher.
4. Put the insertion point after the last sentence in your document and press the enter (return) key three times to add some blank lines.
5. Type the following at the end of your document:
   Number of "E-books" found with match case = #
   Number of "e-books" found with match case = #
   Total number of "e-books" found without match case = #
6. Use the find command to replace the **#** with the number of occurrences you find for each set of conditions.
7. Use **Find and Replace** to make the following changes.
   a. Replace "complete" in the second paragraph with "completed".
   b. Replace "portability" in the third paragraph with "mobility".
8. Choose any three words and change them so they are purposely misspelled. They will display as underlined with red dots.
9. Right-click (control-click on Mac) each word and fix the misspellings.
10. Fix any other words which are flagged with a red doted underline. Feel free to add any words marked as misspelled to the dictionary. To do this right-click (control-click on Mac) the word and choose "Add to Dictionary".
11. Read it completely once more and fix any other spelling or grammar errors you find in the document.
12. Print your final document (or share it as directed by your teacher).
13. If your final document prints on two pages, be sure to staple them together before turning it in. Close the document's tab and move it to your class folder.

E-books Supercharge Reading

E-books, or electronic books, are becoming more and more popular these days. E-book reader devices like the Nook from Barnes and Noble and Amazon's line of Kindle products are becoming increasingly common. These devices have many features students and consumers have found very useful.

First, the 2012 models can hold anywhere from 1,000 and 3,500 books, all at your fingertips. They are lightweight, weighing as little as 6 ounces. E-books can be purchased inexpensively; however e-textbooks remain priced comparably with their expensive printed versions. These e-books can be purchased wirelessly and appear on the device seconds after the purchase is completed. They come in varying sizes as well, with some products offering displays as small as 6 inches or as big as 10 inches. Most of these devices can go weeks without a battery recharge.

In addition to their portability, e-book readers have many features to help those with special needs. Text sizes can be increased at will to help visually challenged readers. Some e-readers support audible reading of the text to help those with sight issues.

Some e-book readers are now providing other features, such as calendar and mail applications and the ability to play games purchased electronically and cheaply. Apple's iPad was the first to offer such features. The iPad, a tablet with e-reader functionality, was announced in 2010 and has remained dominant in the tablet market ever since. Other manufacturers offer less expensive options but with fewer features and/or decreased performance when compared to the iPad.

These e-readers have made the activity of reading more mobile and convenient. While retail bookstore chains are challenged to keep their doors open, e-readers are bringing the store to consumers. Lawrence Clark Powell once said:

"We are the children of a technological age. We have found streamlined ways of doing much of our routine work. Printing is no longer the only way of reproducing books. Reading them, however, has not changed."

It won't be long before heavy school textbooks are replaced with e-readers holding all the information they could ever need in one small device.

Number of "E-books" found with match case on= #
Number of "e-books" found with match case on = #
Total number of "e-books" found without match case = #

Lesson WP4

Lesson WP4.1 - Ways to Select Text

Lesson 4 is in two parts -- WP4.1 and WP4.2. After completing both parts, you will be ready for **Opportunity WP4.**

Word processors would be of little use if we couldn't change and manipulate the text we have entered into our document.

Cut, Copy and Paste are three of the most used word processing commands. These commands work together to help you copy, move or remove text in your document. Before we talk about these skills (covered in Lesson WP4.2), we need to learn about the various ways to **select** the text you want to work with. That is our topic for Lesson WP4.1.

Selecting text

There are three methods for **selecting** (or **highlighting**) a portion of text in your document-- dragging through the text, using shift-click, and using your arrows while holding down shift. You can also select an entire paragraph or even all text in your document at once. We'll practice these highlighting methods in this lesson.

First, let's open the **Promotion** document from your Google Drive. **Make a copy** (File menu) of this file and name it **Promotion WP4**. We covered these commands in Lesson WP1.

A group of highlighted text is also called a **text block** .For steps 1-5, you can choose ANY text in your document. It's your choice. We will not make any changes to the document at this time.

1. Highlight by **dragging through the text**
    a. Point your I-beam mouse pointer to the left of the first word you want to select. [5]
    b. Click and drag your mouse through the text to the end of your desired text block.
    c. Release the mouse button when you have reached the end of your desired text.
    d. Click anywhere outside your selected text block to de-select your text.
    e. Repeat steps 1a-d two more times in another part of your document for practice.

---

[5] The I-beam pointer was introduced in the Getting Started lesson.

2. Highlight by **clicking and shift-clicking**
    a. Choose another block of text to select.
    b. Click your I-beam mouse pointer to the left of the first word you want to select.
    c. Now, **shift-click**[6] the I-beam pointer to the right of the last word you want to select.
    d. Release the shift key.
    e. Click anywhere outside your selected text block to de-select your text.
    f. Repeat steps 2a-e two more times in another part of your document for practice.

3. Highlight using the **shift and arrow keys**
    a. Point your I-beam mouse pointer to the <u>left</u> of the <u>first</u> word you want to select.
    b. While holding down the **shift** key, use the four arrow keys (← ↑ → ↓) to highlight your desired block of text. The up and down arrows add or subtract a line at a time from your text block. The left and right arrows add or subtract a letter at a time.
    c. Release the shift key when you are done with your selection.
    d. Click anywhere outside your selected text block to de-select your text.
    e. Repeat steps 3a-c two more times in another part of your document for practice.

4. Highlight a word instantly
    a. Pick a word to select.
    b. **Double-click** the I-beam mouse point on the word.
    c. Your word is now selected.
    d. Click anywhere outside your selected text block to de-select your text.
    e. Repeat steps 4a-d two more times in another part of your document for practice.

5. Highlight an entire paragraph instantly
    a. Pick a paragraph to select
    b. **Triple-click** the I-beam mouse point on the word
    c. Your paragraph is now selected
    d. Click anywhere outside your selected text block to de-select your text.
    e. Repeat steps 5a-d two more times in another part of your document for practice.

6. Select your entire document
    a. If at any time you want to make a change to the entire document at once, you can simply highlight all the text. Here's how:
        i. Click on Google's Drive's **Edit** menu.
        ii. Choose **Select All...** from the menu.
        iii. Click anywhere outside your selected text block to de-select your text.

---

[6] **Shift-click:** Hold down the shift key and click.

Google Drive Essentials, George Somers

Lesson WP4.2 - Cut, Copy, & Paste and Drag and Drop Editing

Cut, Copy and Paste are three of the most used word processing commands. These commands work together to help you copy, move or remove text in your document. Understanding how they work is essential to being able to successfully work with the text in your document. When used with the text selection skills covered in Lesson 4.1, you can easily manipulate the text in your document.

Additionally, we'll learn about **drag and drop editing**. Drag and drop editing is a way that you can move text blocks from one location to another in your document by simply selecting and dragging your text block to where you want it moved.

We'll also be learning about your computer's **clipboard**. The **clipboard** is an area in the computer's memory which temporarily holds text when using the **copy** and **cut** commands. Anytime you select a text block and either **copy** or **cut** that text, the selected text is stored in the clipboard. Using the **paste** command will take whatever is stored in the clipboard and insert it wherever the insertion point is located.

Finally, we'll learn about the **Undo** and **Redo** commands. **Undo** is used to undo the step you just did. It is a great way to undo something you did but aren't sure what you did or how you did it. **Redo** is used to undo your **Undo** if you decide you liked it better before.

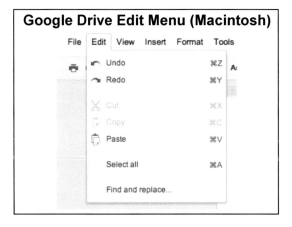
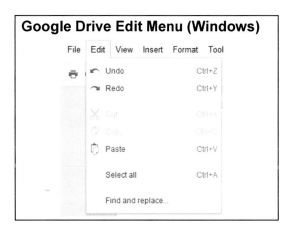

Since these commands are used so frequently, you will also want to learn their **keyboard shortcuts**. They are listed next to the command name in the Edit menu. The Google Drive **Edit** menu is shown above (Mac computer version shown on the left above, the Windows version is on the right above). Make a note of these keyboard shortcuts to use later.

Ready to practice these commands? Let's go!!

With the **Promotion WP4** still open, complete the following steps to learn about these time-saving commands.

1. Locate the paragraph that begins with "We invite you to come see a demonstration…"
2. Position the insertion point after the word "demonstration" by clicking your I-beam pointer (see right) just before the word that follows it. We will add some text here.
3. After the word "demonstration", type "of the Butler Pad".
4. At the end of the first body paragraph, find the sentence "It's your personal butler!"
5. Using one of the selection methods we learned about in Lesson 4.1, highlight this sentence.
6. Go to Google Drive's **Edit** menu and select **Copy**. A copy of this sentence has been placed in your computer's **clipboard**.
7. Return to the paragraph that begins with "We invite you to come see a demonstration…" At the end of that paragraph, add your copied sentence by selecting **Paste** from the **Edit** menu.[7]
8. Adjust your document as needed so that there is one space between your sentences and only one blank line before the next paragraph.
9. The sentence that is being stored in the clipboard is now pasted (or inserted) at the insertion point's position. In fact, the **clipboard** still holds this sentence.
10. Let's **paste** this sentence somewhere else.
    a. Locate the paragraph that begins with "Enhanced Home Technologies is no stranger to innovation. "
    b. Type the sentence "Now, we are adding the Butler Pad." at the end of this paragraph and add a space after it.
    c. Use **Edit>Paste** to insert the sentence still being stored in the clipboard.

---

[7] If you are prompted to install the Google Copy and Paste plug-in for your browser, let your teacher know and he/she will help you with this.

11. Looking at our document, we now decide that the last sentence ("It's your personal Butler.") is used too much. Select this sentence and use **Edit>Cut** to remove it.[8]
12. We also decide that it would be better to have the second body paragraph ("Today, Bart Stone has built Enhanced Home Technologies...") after the one that begins "Enhanced Home Technologies is no stranger..." because we should summarize the company's history before talking about its present. In the next few steps, we'll move this paragraph using **Cut** and **Paste**.
    a. Select (highlight) the entire second body paragraph ("Today, Bart Stone has built Enhanced Home Technologies...") by **triple-clicking** it.
    b. Go to the **Edit** menu and choose the **Cut** command. This paragraph is now removed from your document. But don't worry! It is stored temporarily in your computer's **clipboard**.
    c. Place the insertion point before the paragraph that begins "We invite you to come see ..." and choose **Paste** from the **Edit** menu. The paragraph that you cut is now inserted before this paragraph and our paragraphs are now in proper order.
    d. Once again, adjust your document as needed so that there is one space between your sentences and only one blank line before the next paragraph.
13. Now, let's practice with the **Undo** and **Redo**.
    a. Let's pretend we wanted to see your paragraphs in their original order. Select **undo** from the edit menu (or use the keyboard shortcut) a few times until the paragraphs are back where they were. You may need to do **Edit>Undo** three or four times to undo all your steps and get them back to their original order.
    b. Now, let's pretend we want them back to the new order. Use **Edit>Redo** a few times until the paragraph order is now in the new order The paragraph that

---

[8] Optionally, you could highlight the paragraph and press the **backspace** key (**delete** on Mac computers) to remove the text.

begins with the words "Enhanced Home Technologies is no stranger… "should be followed by the paragraph that begins "Today, Bart Stone has built .."

    c. Repeat step 13a until the paragraphs are back to their original order using the **Undo** command.

14. Now we'll learn another way to move paragraphs using a method called **Drag and Drop Editing**. Here's how:

    a. Select the paragraph that begins "Enhanced Home Technologies is no stranger…"

    b. Point your mouse to the middle of your selection but don't click.

    c. We are now going to move this paragraph by dragging. To do this, hold your mouse button down and move your I-beam to the location in your document where you want your paragraph to <u>begin</u>, just before the paragraph that begins with the words "We invite you".

    d. Release the button and your paragraph will again be moved before this paragraph.

    e. Once again, adjust your document as needed so that there is one space between your sentences and only one blank line before the next paragraph.

Your document in its completed form is shown on the last page of this lesson. Make sure your document matches before continuing with **Opportunity WP4.** Close this document and move it to your class folder in Google Drive.

You are now ready for **Opportunity WP4**.

Let's review!

To make a **copy** of a text block,

1. Select your text block.
2. From the **Edit** menu, choose **Copy**.
3. Move the insertion point to the place in the document where you want your copy of that text to be.
4. From the **Edit** menu, choose **Paste**.
5. The original text block remains in its original location and a copy is placed at the location of the insertion point.

To **move** the text block, use the same procedure but use the **Cut** and **Paste** commands. The original text block is now removed and relocated somewhere else in your document.

Also, practice your keyboard shortcuts! They will save you a lot of time in the as you work on your documents.

You are now ready for **Opportunity WP4**.

AT THE END OF THIS LESSON, YOUR DOCUMENT SHOULD LOOK LIKE THIS...

Dear Preferred Customer;

Today, we are introducing a technology product that will blow your mind. The new Butler Pad from Enhanced Home Technologies will serve all your home automation needs. From turning on your lights to setting your lawn sprinkler system, the Butler Pad is literally at your command. Simply use your voice to control all aspects of your Butler Pad system. It's your personal butler!

Enhanced Home Technologies is no stranger to innovation. From its founding in 1997 by technology visionary Bart Stone, Enhanced Home Technologies has been a leader in household electronics. That same year, he launched his first home product, the digital picture frame. In 2000, we introduced the world's first internet-connected thermostat. That product was followed by the first Internet-connected refrigerator and microwave in 2005. Now, we are adding the Butler Pad.

Today, Bart Stone has built Enhanced Home Technologies into an international home technology leader. With over 100 life-changing products and over 1250 patents, Enhanced Home Technologies has more than 20 offices worldwide. Its products are found in 5-star hotels and mansions of the rich and famous. Now, we are taking advantage of more efficient manufacturing processes to make this technology affordable for every family.

We invite you to come see a demonstration of the Butler Pad at a local home improvement store near you. Once you see this home automation system in action, you will never know how you lived without it. Not only is it convenient, but it will learn your living habits and save you money on your electrical bill in the process. It's your personal butler!

You can visit our website, http://enhanced-home-technologies.com for video demonstrations of our line of products. You can also find product, pricing, and contact information there.

Sincerely,

<Student Name>
Residential Technologies Unit

P.S. Order in the next two weeks and you'll get a free consultation and save 15% on a new Butler Pad system. Don't miss out on this great opportunity. You'll be saving money now to lower your energy bills later.

Opportunity WP4:

Cut, Copy, & Paste and Drag and Drop Editing

Follow the steps below to produce the document as displayed on the next page. The purpose of this assignment is to give you the opportunity to show what you learned from the lesson. If allowed by your teacher, you can refer to the lesson pages to refresh your memory.

1. Log into Google Drive and **open Opportunity WP1** from your class folder.
2. **Make a copy** and name the document **Opportunity WP4** or a variation as directed by your teacher.
3. Type or edit your assignment header (name, assignment, date, subject, etc.) as directed by your teacher.
4. Highlight the text found in the second paragraph as shown below:

> First, the 2012 models can hold anywhere from 1,000 and 3,500 books, all at your fingertips. They are lightweight, weighing as little as 6 ounces. E-books can be purchased inexpensively, however e-textbooks remain priced comparably with their expensive printed versions. These e-books can be purchased wirelessly and appear on the device seconds after the purchase is complete.They come in varying sizes as well, with some products offering displays as small as 6 inches or as big as 10 inches. Most of these devices can go weeks without a battery recharge.

5. Use **Cut and Paste** to make this its own paragraph below the second paragraph as a new third paragraph (see result on next page).
6. **Undo** the Paste. Press **UNDO** (2 or 3 times) again as needed until the text block again looks like the figure above.
7. Now move the same text block using the drag-and-drop method.
8. If needed, add a blank line before and after the new paragraph to match the result on the next page.
9. At the end of your document, add two blank lines by pressing the enter (return) key three times after the last sentence in your document.
10. Highlight the title "E-books Supercharge Reading". Use **Copy and Paste** to add this text to the end of your document.
11. Press enter (return) again to start to new line of text.
12. Add your first and last name to the end of the document.
13. Read it completely once more and fix any other spelling or grammar errors you find in the document. Make sure it matches what is shown on the next page.
14. Print your final document (or share it as directed by your teacher).
15. Close the document's tab and move it to your class folder.

E-books Supercharge Reading

E-books, or electronic books, are becoming more and more popular these days. E-book reader devices like the Nook from Barnes and Noble and Amazon's line of Kindle products are becoming increasingly common. These devices have many features students and consumers have found very useful.

First, the 2012 models can hold anywhere from 1,000 and 3,500 books, all at your fingertips. They are lightweight, weighing as little as 6 ounces. They come in varying sizes as well, with some products offering displays as small as 6 inches or as big as 10 inches. Most of these devices can go weeks without a battery recharge.

E-books can be purchased inexpensively, however e-textbooks remain priced comparably with their expensive printed versions. These e-books can be purchased wirelessly and appear on the device seconds after the purchase is complete.

In addition to their portability, e-book readers have many features to help those with special needs. Text sizes can be increased at will to help visually challenged readers. Some e-readers support audible reading of the text to help those with sight issues.

Some e-book readers are now providing other features, such as calendar and mail applications and the ability to play games purchased electronically and cheaply. Apple's iPad was the first to offer such features. The iPad, a tablet with e-reader functionality, was announced in 2010 and has remained dominant in the tablet market ever since. Other manufacturers offer less expensive options but with fewer features and/or decreased performance when compared to the iPad.

These e-readers have made the activity of reading more mobile and convenient. While retail bookstore chains are challenged to keep their doors open, e-readers are bringing the store to consumers. Lawrence Clark Powell once said:

"We are the children of a technological age. We have found streamlined ways of doing much of our routine work. Printing is no longer the only way of reproducing books. Reading them, however, has not changed."

It won't be long before heavy school textbooks are replaced with e-readers holding all the information they could ever need in one small device.

E-books Supercharge Reading
<Student Name>

Lesson WP5 - Working with Fonts

The term **fonts** refers to the shape of the text we type, whether it be letters, numbers or special characters or symbols. Some fonts, like Arial are plainer. Fonts like *Corona* and Crafty are fancier with extra details that hang off the letters. Fancier letters are great for headings and titles. Plainer fonts are better for paragraphs like this one.

Font sizes are measured in pixels (or dots) in height. We also refer to pixels as **points**. A capital letter that in 72 points is size will print one inch high.

This text size is 72 points.

This text size is 36 points size.

A more typical font size, like this one, is 11 points.

Font styles can also be applied to fonts - like **bold**, *italics*, underlined, colors or ***all four***. For example, book titles, like *Harry Potter and the Sorcerer's Stone* by J.K. Rowling are often italicized. You will see all of these styles used throughout this book.

Google Drive's menu bar (left side)

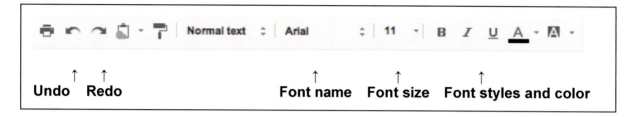

Fonts, sizes and styles can all be changed from Google Drive's button bar (above). The default (or normal) font settings are Arial 11 with no styles applied. You can change your font by clicking on the name of the font (e.g. Arial) and selecting the new font from the menu that appears. You can change the font size by clicking on the size number (e.g. 11) and selecting your new size from the menu. You can also type in any number between 6 and 400 where the 11 normally appears to change to that size.

Additionally, **font styles** can be turned on and off by clicking the font style buttons on the button bar. The **B** is for bold, *I* is for italics, and the U is for underline. You can choose to have one, two, or three styles applied to your text. The button to the right of the underline button is for changing text colors. We'll be playing with those also in this lesson.

Keep in mind that you can make font changes before you type the text or you can select your text and make any changes to already existing text. In this way, you can focus initially on the text of your document and then go back later to make any font setting changes. Word processing features, like font settings, can be changed anytime. I recommend you get your text in first, then apply font changes.

As with the commands learned in Lesson WP4, there are keyboard shortcuts for the bold, italics and underline commands. Practice them and they will save you time. They are as follows:

Command	Windows Shortcut	Macintosh Shortcut
Bold	CTRL-B	CMD-B (or ⌘-**B**)
Italics	CTRL-I	CMD-I (or ⌘-**I**)
Underline	CTRL-U	CMD-U (or ⌘-**U**)

In the following steps, you'll change the font settings in a document based on the Promotion letter. For our practice, you can choose which text you want to change.

So, here we go!

1. First, let's open the **Promotion** document from your Google Drive.
2. **Make a copy** (File menu) of this file and name it **Fonts WP5.** We covered these commands in Lesson WP1.
3. Highlight the entire second paragraph which begins with the words "Today, Bart Stone has built..." by triple-clicking it.
4. Click the **bold** button on the button bar to make this paragraph bold.
5. With this paragraph still selected, click to **bold** button to turn off bold. (It works like a light switch!)
6. Click the **bold** button to apply the bold font style to this paragraph again.
7. Click the **italics** button to make it italicized.
8. Click the **underline** button to make this paragraph underlined.
9. Click the **undo** button on the button bar three times to remove the bold, italics and underline styles from this paragraph. *Hint: see figure at top of the previous page.*
10. Click the **redo** button on the button bar three times to re-apply bold, italics and underline back to your paragraph. *Hint: see figure at top of the previous page.*
11. Here's another way to clear all font settings. You can remove all font styles from this paragraph by clicking the **Normal text** button and clicking on the normal text option in the menu. Now all text is back to Arial 11 with no bold, italics or underlined.
12. With body paragraph 2 still selected, choose a color of your choice by clicking on the **Text color** button on the button bar and clicking on a color from the menu that appears.

Now practice with these settings (fonts, sizes, colors and styles) by making each paragraph in your letter a different font, size, color and style. What you choose is up to you. Go at it and have fun!

Close this document and move it to your class folder in Google Drive.

Great job! You are now ready for **Opportunity WP5.**

Opportunity WP5:

Working with Fonts

Follow the steps below to produce the document as displayed on the next page. The purpose of this assignment is to give you the opportunity to show what you learned from the lesson. If allowed by your teacher, you can refer to the lesson pages to refresh your memory.

1. Log into Google Drive and **open Opportunity WP1** from your class folder.

2. **Make a copy** and name the document **Opportunity WP5** or a variation as directed by your teacher.

3. Type or edit your assignment header (name, assignment, date, subject, etc.) as directed by your teacher.

4. Use the directions on the next page to change the **fonts**, **font sizes** and **styles** as indicated.

5. Read it completely once more and fix any other spelling or grammar errors you find in the document. Make sure it matches what is shown on the next page.

6. Print your final document (or share it as directed by your teacher).

7. Close the document's tab and move it to your class folder.

E-books Supercharge Reading *(Crafty Girls 18, Bold, Underlined)*

E-books, or electronic books, are becoming more and more popular these days. E-book reader devices like the Nook from Barnes and Noble and Amazon's line of Kindle products are becoming increasingly common. These devices have many features students and consumers have found very useful. *(Syncopate 12)*

First, the 2012 models can hold anywhere from 1,000 and 3,500 books, all at your fingertips. They are lightweight, weighing as little as 6 ounces. E-books can be purchased inexpensively, however e-textbooks remain priced comparable with their expensive printed versions. These e-books can be purchased wirelessly and appear on the device seconds after the purchase is complete. They come in varying sizes as well, with some products offering displays as small as 6 inches or as big as 10 inches. Most of these devices can go weeks without a battery recharge. *(Times New Roman)*

In addition to their portability, e-book readers have many features to help those with special needs. Text sizes can be increased at will to help visually challenged readers. Some e-readers support audible reading of the text to help those with sight issues. *(Arial 18 — "Text sizes can be increased")*

Some e-book readers are now providing other features, such as calendar and mail applications and the ability to play games purchased electronically and cheaply. Apple's iPad was the first to offer such features. The iPad, a tablet with e-reader functionality, was announced in 2010 and has remained dominant in the tablet market ever since. Other manufacturers offer less expensive options but with fewer features and/or decreased performance when compared to the iPad.

These e-readers have made the activity of reading more mobile and convenient. While retail bookstore chains are challenged to keep their doors open, e-readers are bringing the store to consumers. Lawrence Clark Powell once said:

"We are the children of a technological age. We have found streamlined ways of doing much of our routine work. Printing is no longer the only way of reproducing books. Reading them, however, has not changed." *(Italic)*

It won't be long before heavy school textbooks are replaced with e-readers holding all the information they could ever need in one small device.

Lesson WP6 - Paragraph Indents

In this lesson, we'll cover paragraph **indents.** First, you'll learn how indents change the way your paragraph works, then we'll practice them. Of course, you'll be using these new skills in **Opportunity WP6** to show your teacher what you have learned.

There are three kinds of paragraph indents -- **left**, **right**, and **first line**. Each paragraph can have different settings as required. Below are the three kinds of indents illustrated for you.

> This paragraph has been indented on the left side, meaning that there is additional space between it and the left margin. Text wrap is still handled the same way so there is no need to press return at the end of each line.

>> "This paragraph has been indented on the left side AND the right side, meaning that there is additional space between it and the left and right margins. This is the typical way a long quote is used in a research paper. The entire quote is made to be its own paragraph and quotation marks are put at the beginning and end of the paragraph."

>   This paragraph has a first line indent, meaning that there is additional space between it and the left margin but only for the first line. Text wrap is still handled the same way so there is no need to press return at the end of each line.

When the first line of text begins farther to the left than the rest of the paragraph, it is called a **hanging indent.** Text wrap is still handled the same way so there is no need to press return at the end of each line. The right indent is unchanged.

These indent settings are made on your ruler bar (see figure below). The small blue rectangle, usually at zero on the ruler bar, is the location of the first line indent. The down-pointing triangle below it is the setting for the left paragraph indent. The down-pointing triangle, usually at the 6.5 inch mark on the ruler, is the right indent setting. To change each of these settings, simply drag the indent markers to their desired location. Changes will affect the paragraph where the insertion point is.

↑
First line (top) and left indent (bottom) markers

↑
Right indent marker

Now it's your turn...

1. First, let's open the **Promotion** document from your Google Drive.
2. **Make a copy** (File menu) of this file and name it **Promotion WP6.** We covered these commands in **Lesson WP1**.
3. For the first body paragraph (the one that begins "*Today, we are introducing...*), drag the **first line indent** to the half-inch mark on the ruler.
4. For the next paragraph, move the **left indent** marker to 1.5 inches on the ruler. Then move the right indent marker for the same paragraph to the 5 inch location on the ruler.
5. For the next paragraph ("*Enhanced Home Technologies...*"), move the **left indent** marker to 1 inch on the ruler and the **first line indent** marker back to zero to create a **hanging indent**.
6. Finally, to make this letter fit on one page, delete one of the blank lines before the **complimentary close** ("*Sincerely,*").
7. It should now look like the letter on the next page. If it doesn't, make the necessary adjustments so that it does.
8. Close this document and move it to your class folder in Google Drive.

You are now ready to proceed with **Opportunity WP6**.

Dear Preferred Customer;

      Today, we are introducing a technology product that will blow your mind. The new Butler Pad from Enhanced Home Technologies will serve all your home automation needs. From turning on your lights to setting your lawn sprinkler system, the Butler Pad is literally at your command. Simply use your voice to control all aspects of your Butler Pad system. It's your personal butler!

      Today, Bart Stone has built Enhanced Home Technologies into an international home technology leader. With over 100 life-changing products and over 1250 patents, Enhanced Home Technologies has more than 20 offices worldwide. Its products are found in 5-star hotels and mansions of the rich and famous. Now, we are taking advantage of more efficient manufacturing processes to make this technology affordable for every family.

      Enhanced Home Technologies is no stranger to innovation. From its founding in 1997 by technology visionary Bart Stone, Enhanced Home Technologies has been a leader in household electronics. That same year, he launched his first home product, the digital picture frame. In 2000, we introduced the world's first internet-connected thermostat. That product was followed by the first Internet-connected refrigerator and microwave in 2005.

We invite you to come see a demonstration at a local home improvement store near you. Once you see this home automation system in action, you will never know how you lived without it. Not only is it convenient, but it will learn your living habits and save you money on your electrical bill in the process.

You can visit our website, http://enhanced-home-technologies.com for video demonstrations of our line of products. You can also find product, pricing, and contact information there.

Sincerely,

<Student Name>
Residential Technologies Unit

P.S. Order in the next two weeks and you'll get a free consultation and save 15% on a new Butler Pad system. Don't miss out on this great opportunity. You'll be saving money now to lower your energy bills later.

Opportunity WP6:

Paragraph Indents

Follow the steps below to produce the document as displayed on the next page. The purpose of this assignment is to give you the opportunity to show what you learned from the lesson. If allowed by your teacher, you can refer to the lesson pages to refresh your memory.

1. Log into Google Drive and **open Opportunity WP1** from your class folder.
2. **Make a copy** and name the document **Opportunity WP6** or a variation as directed by your teacher.
3. Type or edit your assignment header (name, assignment, date, subject, etc.) as directed by your teacher.
4. Indent the first three paragraphs one half inch.
5. Set a half-inch hanging indent for the fifth paragraph ("These e-readers have made…").
6. Indent the sixth paragraph ("We are the children…) one inch on the left and right sides.
7. Check your document against the document as displayed on the next page. They should match.
8. Read it completely once more and fix any other spelling or grammar errors you find in the document. Make sure it matches what is shown on the next page.
9. Print your final document (or share it as directed by your teacher).
10. Close the document's tab and move it to your class folder.

E-books Supercharge Reading

      E-books, or electronic books, are becoming more and more popular these days. E-book reader devices like the Nook from Barnes and Noble and Amazon's line of Kindle products are becoming increasingly common. These devices have many features students and consumers have found very useful.

      First, the 2012 models can hold anywhere from 1,000 and 3,500 books, all at your fingertips. They are lightweight, weighing as little as 6 ounces. E-books can be purchased inexpensively, however e-textbooks remain priced comparably with their expensive printed versions. These e-books can be purchased wirelessly and appear on the device seconds after the purchase is complete. They come in varying sizes as well, with some products offering displays as small as 6 inches or as big as 10 inches. Most of these devices can go weeks without a battery recharge.

      In addition to their portability, e-book readers have many features to help those with special needs. Text sizes can be increased at will to help visually challenged readers. Some e-readers support audible reading of the text to help those with sight issues.

Some e-book readers are now providing other features, such as calendar and mail applications and the ability to play games purchased electronically and cheaply. Apple's iPad was the first to offer such features. The iPad, a tablet with e-reader functionality, was announced in 2010 and has remained dominant in the tablet market ever since. Other manufacturers offer less expensive options but with fewer features and/or decreased performance when compared to the iPad.

These e-readers have made the activity of reading more mobile and convenient. While retail
      bookstore chains are challenged to keep their doors open, e-reader are bringing the
      store to consumers. Lawrence Clark Powell once said:

> "We are the children of a technological age. We have found
> streamlined ways of doing much of our routine work. Printing is no
> longer the only way of reproducing books. Reading them,
> however, has not changed."

It won't be long before heavy school textbooks are replaced with e-readers holding all the information they could ever need in one small device.

Lesson WP7 - Paragraph Line Spacing

Line spacing refers to the vertical spacing of a paragraph. Line spacing can make documents with a lot of text easier to read by adding white space to the page. Normal (default) line spacing is 1.15 and is slightly more than single spaced (or 1.0). **Single-spaced** means that there is no extra space between each line of your paragraph. Double spacing (or 2.0) adds the equivalent of one line height between each line of text.

Here are some examples:

This is a **single-spaced** paragraph. There is no additional space between the lines of your paragraph. This is a single-spaced paragraph. Plus, as you type, Google Docs creates a new line of text for you automatically thanks to word wrap. There is no need to press enter (return) at the end of each line of text to begin a new line.

This is a double-spaced paragraph. There is a blank line of space between each line of your

paragraph. However you do not have to skip lines manually. Simply set your line spacing for

double-space and Google Drive does the rest. There is no need to press enter (or return) at the

end of each line. Just let text-wrap work as usual and skip lines automatically.

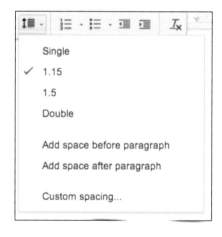

For more of a compromise between these two settings, the default is set to 1.15 spacing, which is the setting used by most of the paragraphs in this book.

For a little more space you might try 1.5 spacing which adds the equivalent of a half-line of space between each line, like this one does. For example, if you are using a 24 point size font, Google Drive automatically adds 12 points of blank space between each line.

When doing research papers and other assignments for your teachers, they may specify which line space setting to use. Now, you know how.

The line spacing menu is found on the right end of the Google Drive button bar. Shown above, the line spacing menu shows you your available options. There are also options for adding a line of space before or after your paragraphs.

So let's get started...

1. First, let's open the **Promotion** document from your Google Drive.

2. **Make a copy** (File menu) of this file and name it **Promotion WP7**. We covered these commands in **Lesson WP1**.

3. Click the insertion point anywhere in the first body paragraph (the one that begins "*Today, we are introducing...*) and set the line spacing menu to **Double**.

4. Change the second body paragraph ("Today, Bart Stone...") and make the line spacing **Single**.

5. For the paragraph that begins with "We invite you to come ...", make the line spacing **1.5**.

6. Your document should now look like the letter on the next page. If it doesn't, make the necessary adjustments so that it does.

7. Close this document and move it to your class folder in Google Drive.

Congratulations, you are now ready for **Opportunity WP7**.

Dear Preferred Customer;

Today, we are introducing a technology product that will blow your mind. The new Butler Pad from Enhanced Home Technologies will serve all your home automation needs. From turning on your lights to setting your lawn sprinkler system, the Butler Pad is literally at your command. Simply use your voice to control all aspects of your Butler Pad system. It's your personal butler!

Today, Bart Stone has built Enhanced Home Technologies into an international home technology leader. With over 100 life-changing products and over 1250 patents, Enhanced Home Technologies has more than 20 offices worldwide. Its products are found in 5-star hotels and mansions of the rich and famous. Now, we are taking advantage of more efficient manufacturing processes to make this technology affordable for every family.

Enhanced Home Technologies is no stranger to innovation. From its founding in 1997 by technology visionary Bart Stone, Enhanced Home Technologies has been a leader in household electronics. That same year, he launched his first home product, the digital picture frame. In 2000, we introduced the world's first internet-connected thermostat. That product was followed by the first Internet-connected refrigerator and microwave in 2005.

We invite you to come see a demonstration at a local home improvement store near you. Once you see this home automation system in action, you will never know how you lived without it. Not only is it convenient, but it will learn your living habits and save you money on your electrical bill in the process.

You can visit our website, http://enhanced-home-technologies.com for video demonstrations of our line of products. You can also find product, pricing, and contact information there.

Sincerely,

<Student Name>
Residential Technologies Unit

P.S. Order in the next two weeks and you'll get a free consultation and save 15% on a new Butler Pad system. Don't miss out on this great opportunity. You'll be saving money now to lower your energy bills later.

Opportunity WP7

Paragraph Line Spacing

Follow the steps below to produce the document as displayed on the next page. The purpose of this assignment is to give you the opportunity to show what you learned from the lesson. If allowed by your teacher, you can refer to the lesson pages to refresh your memory.

1. Log into Google Drive and **open Opportunity WP1** from your class folder.
2. **Make a copy** and name the document **Opportunity WP7** or a variation as directed by your teacher.
3. Type or edit your assignment header (name, assignment, date, subject, etc.) as directed by your teacher.
4. Make the first paragraph **Double** line spacing.
5. Set the second paragraph to **Single** line spacing.
6. Set the third paragraph to **1.5** line spacing.
7. Set all other paragraphs to **Single** line spacing.
8. Check your document against the document as displayed on the next page. They should match.
9. Read it completely once more and fix any other spelling or grammar errors you find in the document. Make sure it matches what is shown on the next page.
10. Print your final document (or share it as directed by your teacher).
11. Close the document's tab and move it to your class folder.

E-books Supercharge Reading

E-books, or electronic books, are becoming more and more popular these days. E-book reader devices like the Nook from Barnes and Noble and Amazon's line of Kindle products are becoming increasingly common. These devices have many features students and consumers have found very useful.

First, the 2012 models can hold anywhere from 1,000 and 3,500 books, all at your fingertips. They are lightweight, weighing as little as 6 ounces. E-books can be purchased inexpensively, however e-textbooks remain priced comparable with their expensive printed versions. These e-books can be purchased wirelessly and appear on the device seconds after the purchase is complete. They come in varying sizes as well, with some products offering displays as small as 6 inches or as big as 10 inches. Most of these devices can go weeks without a battery recharge.

In addition to their portability, e-book readers have many features to help those with special needs. Text sizes can be increased at will to help visually challenged readers. Some e-readers support audible reading of the text to help those with sight issues.

Some e-book readers are now providing other features, such as calendar and mail applications and the ability to play games purchased electronically and cheaply. Apple's iPad was the first to offer such features. The iPad, a tablet with e-reader functionality, was announced in 2010 and has remained dominant in the tablet market ever since. Other manufacturers offer less expensive options but with fewer features and/or decreased performance when compared to the iPad.

These e-readers have made the activity of reading more mobile and convenient. While retail bookstore chains are challenged to keep their doors open, e-readers are bringing the store to consumers. Lawrence Clark Powell once said:

"We are the children of a technological age. We have found streamlined ways of doing much of our routine work. Printing is no longer the only way of reproducing books. Reading them, however, has not changed."

It won't be long before heavy school textbooks are replaced with e-readers holding all the information they could ever need in one small device.

Lesson WP8 - Paragraph Justification

In the last chapter, we learned about line spacing and other adjustments you can make to affect the vertical spacing of paragraphs. Now, we will learn about the horizontal spacing changes you can make to paragraphs. This type of change is known as the **justification** or **alignment** of a paragraph. There are four kinds of justifications which can be applied to a paragraph -- **left**, **right**, **center** and **justified** (or **full justification**). The buttons to make these changes, in that order from left to right, are below.

Allow me to show you some examples before we practice with them.

This is a **left aligned** paragraph. Each line of this paragraph begins at the left margin. The last word of each line does not stop at the same point. The right side of this paragraph will appear jagged. Left aligned paragraphs are the normal (default) setting for paragraphs in all word processors.

This is a **right aligned** paragraph. It is opposite of left alignment. Each line of this paragraph ends at the right margin. It will have the same amount of words on each line but only the end of each line aligns with the right margin, making the left side of this paragraph jagged. Right alignment is typically used for putting something in the upper right or bottom right corner of your paper, such as for your name on a class paper or a page number in the footer. It is not typically used for paragraphs which are more than a single line.

This is a **center aligned** paragraph. Each line is perfectly centered between the left and right margins. If your margins are equal and you folded your paper lengthwise down the middle, each line has the same amount of text on the left side of the center fold and on the right side of the fold. You will also notice that neither the left nor right sides of the paragraph align with the margins. **Center alignment** is often used for signs and single-line paragraphs, like a title. Centering a title means you don't have to use spaces or tabs in an attempt to find the center of the page. The computer will do the calculations for you to ensure that your title is perfectly centered with the click of a button.

Finally, this paragraph is **justified**. This means that each line, with the exception of the last one, begins and ends at the left and right margins. This makes the paragraph look organized and well thought out. The computer adds a little bit of space between each word to make this happen. In actuality, there are no more words in each line than there would be with any other paragraph alignment. This setting is commonly used for legal and official documents.

Ready to see paragraph alignment in action?

1. Once again, let's open the **Promotion** document from your Google Drive.
2. **Make a copy** (File menu) of this file and name it **Promotion WP8.** We covered these commands in **Lesson WP1**.
3. Click your insertion point anywhere in the second body paragraph ("*Today, Bart Stone...*") and make it justified.
4. For the paragraph that begins with "*We invite you to come ...*", make the alignment centered.
5. Put your insertion point at the end of the P.S. paragraph (the last line in the entire document) by clicking after the last word in the paragraph.
6. Press the enter (return) key three times and add some additional lines to your document.
7. Press the align right button on the button bar and type your first and last initials. *(Some offices use a technique like this one to identify the typist of the document)*
8. Your document should now look like the letter on the next page. If it doesn't, make the necessary adjustments so that it does.
9. Close this document and move it to your class folder in Google Drive.

You are now ready for **Opportunity WP8**.

YOUR FINISHED LESSON WP8 SHOULD LOOK LIKE THIS...

Dear Preferred Customer;

Today, we are introducing a technology product that will blow your mind. The new Butler Pad from Enhanced Home Technologies will serve all your home automation needs. From turning on your lights to setting your lawn sprinkler system, the Butler Pad is literally at your command. Simply use your voice to control all aspects of your Butler Pad system. It's your personal butler!

Today, Bart Stone has built Enhanced Home Technologies into an international home technology leader. With over 100 life-changing products and over 1250 patents, Enhanced Home Technologies has more than 20 offices worldwide. Its products are found in 5-star hotels and mansions of the rich and famous. Now, we are taking advantage of more efficient manufacturing processes to make this technology affordable for every family.

Enhanced Home Technologies is no stranger to innovation. From its founding in 1997 by technology visionary Bart Stone, Enhanced Home Technologies has been a leader in household electronics. That same year, he launched his first home product, the digital picture frame. In 2000, we introduced the world's first internet-connected thermostat. That product was followed by the first Internet-connected refrigerator and microwave in 2005.

> We invite you to come see a demonstration at a local home improvement store near you. Once you see this home automation system in action, you will never know how you lived without it. Not only is it convenient, but it will learn your living habits and save you money on your electrical bill in the process.

You can visit our website, http://enhanced-home-technologies.com for video demonstrations of our line of products. You can also find product, pricing, and contact information there.

Sincerely,

<Student Name>
Residential Technologies Unit

P.S. Order in the next two weeks and you'll get a free consultation and save 15% on a new Butler Pad system. Don't miss out on this great opportunity. You'll be saving money now to lower your energy bills later.

<your first and last initials here>

Opportunity WP8

Paragraph Justification

Follow the steps below to produce the document as displayed on the next page. The purpose of this assignment is to give you the opportunity to show what you learned from the lesson. If allowed by your teacher, you can refer to the lesson pages to refresh your memory.

1. Log into Google Drive and **open Opportunity WP1** from your class folder.
2. **Make a copy** and name the document **Opportunity WP8** or a variation as directed by your teacher.
3. Type or edit your assignment header (name, assignment, date, subject, etc.) as directed by your teacher.
4. Make your title **centered**.
5. Make the first two paragraphs **justified** alignment.
6. Make the third and fourth paragraphs **center** aligned.
7. Make the fifth and sixth paragraphs **right** aligned.
8. Check your document against the document as displayed on the next page. They should match.
9. Read it completely once more and fix any other spelling or grammar errors you find in the document. Make sure it matches what is shown on the next page.
10. Print your final document (or share it as directed by your teacher).
11. Close the document's tab and move it to your class folder.

E-books Supercharge Reading

E-books, or electronic books, are becoming more and more popular these days. E-book reader devices like the Nook from Barnes and Noble and Amazon's line of Kindle products are becoming increasingly common. These devices have many features students and consumers have found very useful.

First, the 2012 models can hold anywhere from 1,000 and 3,500 books, all at your fingertips. They are lightweight, weighing as little as 6 ounces. E-books can be purchased inexpensively, however e-textbooks remain priced comparable with their expensive printed versions. These e-books can be purchased wirelessly and appear on the device seconds after the purchase is complete. They come in varying sizes as well, with some products offering displays as small as 6 inches or as big as 10 inches. Most of these devices can go weeks without a battery recharge.

In addition to their portability, e-book readers have many features to help those with special needs. Text sizes can be increased at will to help visually challenged readers. Some e-readers support audible reading of the text to help those with sight issues.

Some e-book readers are now providing other features, such as calendar and mail applications and the ability to play games purchased electronically and cheaply. Apple's iPad was the first to offer such features. The iPad, a tablet with e-reader functionality, was announced in 2010 and has remained dominant in the tablet market ever since. Other manufacturers offer less expensive options but with fewer features and/or decreased performance when compared to the iPad.

These e-readers have made the activity of reading more mobile and convenient. While retail bookstore chains are challenged to keep their doors open, e-readers are bringing the store to consumers. Lawrence Clark Powell once said:

"We are the children of a technological age. We have found streamlined ways of doing much of our routine work. Printing is no longer the only way of reproducing books. Reading them, however, has not changed."

It won't be long before heavy school textbooks are replaced with e-readers holding all the information they could ever need in one small device

Lesson WP9 - Tabs

Tabs provide us the ability to vertically align columns of text. The text in the columns can be set to align up to a specified position on the ruler bar. In addition, Google Drive provides us with three different alignment options -- **left align**, **right align** and **center**. These are not paragraph alignments, however. They are three different ways to align a column of text to a point on the ruler. Here's how they look:

This is a left aligned tab stop set to 1 inch on the ruler. The left side of this column is aligned to 1 inch.	This column is centered to 3.75 inches on the ruler using a center tab stop. Each line is centered to 3.75 inches on the ruler.	This is a right aligned tab stop at 6.5 inches. Each line of this column ends at 6.5 inches on the ruler.

If you don't specify where you want your tab stops to be, the default (or normal) tab stops would be in effect. The default **tab stops** are set to every inch and half-inch on the ruler. For example, 0.5, 1, 1.5, 2, 2.5 and so on. However, they are only left aligned tab stops. If you want different tab stop settings, you will have to do it yourself. Luckily, this is easy to do.

First, you have to know that new tab settings only affect the line the insertion point is on. If you select multiple lines of text, you can set your tabs for all the selected lines at once. Also, pressing the enter (return) key to begin a new line in your document will duplicate the tab settings of the previous line for the newly created line.

To set a new tab stop, click the I-beam pointer anywhere in the line where you want your new tab stop to be. Then click on the ruler to put a tab stop at that point. A pop-up menu will appear. Choose your desired tab stop alignment from that list.

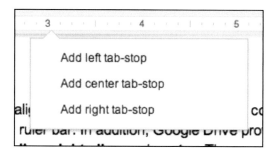

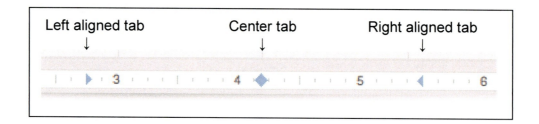

The figure above shows a left aligned tab stop at 2.75 (indicated by the ▷ on the ruler bar), a center tab stop at 4.25 (◆) and a right aligned tab at 5.5 inches (◁). These symbols are called **tab markers.**

If you need to **move** a tab stop, just drag the tab marker left or right to the new position on the ruler bar. It's that easy. Keep in mind, however, that unless you have more than one line of text selected, the tab change will only affect the line where the insertion point is.

Removing a tab stop is just as easy. If you drag the tab marker below the ruler and release the mouse button, the tab stop will be removed. Once again, however, unless you have more than one line of text selected, the tab stop will only be removed for the line where the insertion point is.

Let's give it a whirl!! For this tutorial, you'll be starting a new document from scratch.

1. Go to your Google Drive and from the **New** menu, choose **Document** to start a new document.
2. Go to Google Drive's **File** menu.
3. Name this new file **Tabs WP9**.
4. On the first line, click the **Center Align button** (see at right) to make this line centered.

5. Type the following:

Space Shuttle Data

6. Press the **Enter** key (**Return** on Mac) <u>twice</u> to skip a line.
7. Press the **Left Align button** to continue your document with left paragraph alignment.
8. Click on the one inch mark and choose "Add left tab-stop" to set a 1 inch **left tab-stop** (see right).

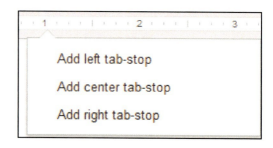

9. Like in Step 8, set a **center tab-stop** at 3.5 inches and a **right tab-stop** at 5.5 inches. Now we have set the tab stops for our table.
10. For the first line of our table do the following:
    a. Press the **Tab** key put the insertion point at the 1-inch tab-stop and then type "*Shuttle Name*"
    b. Press the **Tab** key again and type *First Launch* at the 3.5 inch center tab-stop
    c. Press the Tab key again and type *Longest Flight* at the 5.5 inch right tab-stop
    d. Press the **Enter** key (**Return** on Mac) to start a new line. Take a look at your ruler bar and you will notice that the tab settings are carried over to your new line.

11. Use the instructions from Step 10 to complete the table as follows:

Columbia	April 12, 1981	17 days, 16 hours
Challenger	April 4, 1983	8 days, 5 hours
Discovery	August 30, 1984	15 days, 3 hours
Atlantis	October 3, 1985	13 days, 20 hours
Endeavor	May 7, 1992	16 days, 15 hours

12. Now, double-check your work for accuracy.
13. Looking at our table now, we decide that our second and third columns are a little crowded so we are going to move our 3.5 inch tab stop to 3 inches. Here's how:
    a. Highlight all six lines of your table by dragging your I-beam pointer from the beginning of the first line through the end of the last line. Do not include any lines below your table in your selection.
    b. On the ruler bar, drag the tab-stop marker from 3.5 inches to 3.0 inches.
    c. All the lines of our table should show the middle column centered at 3 inches.
    d. If you have trouble changing all the lines at once, you may need to change each line individually by clicking anywhere in each line, then moving the tab stop. Repeat this step for each line in your table.
14. To wrap up this tutorial, we're going to add a couple of finishing touches.
    a. Highlight your heading "Space Shuttle Data" and make it **bold**.
    b. Highlight the first line of your table and make it **bold**.
    c. Close this document and move it to your class folder in Google Drive.

You are now ready for **Opportunity WP9.**

Opportunity WP9

Tabs

Follow the steps below to produce the document as displayed on the next page. The purpose of this assignment is to give you the opportunity to show what you learned from the lesson. If allowed by your teacher, you can refer to the lesson pages to refresh your memory.

In this Opportunity, you are going to make a word search.

1. Log into Google Drive and create a new document using the **NEW** menu.
2. **Rename** the document **Opportunity WP9** or a variation as directed by your teacher.
3. Type your assignment header (name, assignment, date, subject, etc.) as directed by your teacher.
4. Beginning at 1 inch on the ruler bar, set a center tab stop every quarter inch (every 2 hash marks) until 4 ¼ inches. Your ruler should look like this:

5. Type the word search puzzle as shown on the next page. Press the tab key before typing each letter.
6. Press enter (return) THREE TIMES to add some blank lines after the puzzle.
7. Clear all tabs by dragging all tab markers down and off the ruler bar.
8. Type "Words to Find" and make it **bold**.
9. Press enter (return) TWO TIMES to add a blank line.
10. Set a left tab at 1 inch, a center tab at 3 inches, and a right tab stop at 5 inches at the ruler.
11. Check your document against the document as displayed on the next page. They should match.
12. Read it completely once more and fix any other spelling or grammar errors you find in the document. Make sure it matches what is shown on the next page.
13. Print your final document (or share it as directed by your teacher).
14. Print a second copy and solve the puzzle. If you printed the unsolved puzzle in step 12, staple the solved puzzle to the original and submit them to your teacher. Otherwise turn the solution in to you teacher.
15. Close the document's tab and move it to your class folder.

```
C O M O K A J S I P V G S L
R O F B Z B B F C E I T C J
D R I V E D U K R E M I O E
E T R Z G G T T R A N L D O
H T P E O Q I S B A T T A E
F K A O L C F Y H V C L E M
S B G R A U N W U H I H T R
S L N L O R R F Q G Y I H I
E N R I D B Q R N U C S G S
B I M T G S A M E O V R I E
S D E U P O E L N K S Z R T
W T P O L N L O L Q R Z P F
B X T P T O R Z Z O K A P E
O S V B A T C E S V C M M L
```

Words to Find:

ALIGNMENT	CENTER	COLLABORATE
COLUMNS	DOCS	DRIVE
GOOGLE	LEFT	LOGIN
MARKER	RIGHT	RULER
STOPS	TABS	VERTICAL

Lesson WP10 - Adding a Graphic Object

It is very easy to add a graphic object such as a picture, clip art or line drawing. These images can come from a file on your computer or the Internet. Google Docs makes it very easy to find images which can be used non-commercially so you can avoid any legal issues involving copyright issues. In this lesson, we'll learn how to find and work with images in your document.

Google Docs allows you to search for images from a variety of sources in one, easy-to-use search box and without having to leave Google Docs to download an image to your computer from the Internet. Once an image has been inserted into your document, it can be placed **in-line** with your paragraph text or **fixed** to a specific spot on the page. If you choose fixed, you can drag the image where you want it to be on the page and the text will wrap around it. We'll see how that works in our tutorial.

Let's create a new document in Google Drive. Let's experiment with the **Insert Image** box a bit and see how it works. To bring up this box, go to the **Insert** menu in Google Docs and choose **Image**. The box will look like the following.

The options on the left are to indicate the source of your image. You can **Upload** an image from your computer or **Take a snapshot** using your computer's camera. You can also get images **By URL** (Uniform Resource Locator) if you enter (or copy/paste) the direct web address to an image that lives on the Internet. If you use Google's Picasa Albums you can select **Your albums** and navigate to the desired image. If you choose Google Drive, you can find an image from your Google Drive storage area. **Search**, the last option, allows you to search the Internet for images which have no copyright restrictions concerning its use.

The search option also gives you additional options for searching for images by **Any Type, Faces, Photo, Clip Art** and **Line Drawing**. **Clip Art** have limited colors and can be sized up better than other images found on the Internet. After your initial search, you can narrow down your search using the type options and colors found in the image using the color boxes at the top of the box.

Experiment:

Open a new Google Docs document and rename it **Experiment WP10**.

Go to the **Insert** menu and choose **Image**.

Click on **search** on the left side and enter some words in the search box. Be sure to keep it appropriate. Try narrowing your search by changing the **type** and **color** options. Spend a couple of minutes to see how these options affect your search results. When you are done experimenting, click the **Cancel** button at the bottom of the box.

Now, let's get started with our tutorial...

1. Open the **Tabs WP9** document from your Google Drive.
2. **Make a copy** (File menu) of this file name it **Images WP10.** *We covered these commands in Lesson WP1.*
3. Highlight the title "Space Shuttle Data" and increase the font size to **24**.
4. Press the right arrow button on your keyboard (→) one time to move the cursor to the end of the title line.
5. Press the **Enter** key (**Return** on Macs) **TWO TIMES** to insert a line. Your insertion point should still be centered.
6. From the insert menu, choose **Image...** (*see right*)

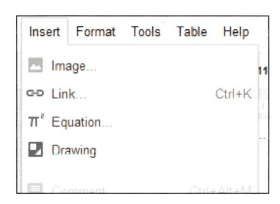

7. On the left side of this box, click on **Search**.
8. In the search box at the top, type "space shuttle" and click the search button (magnifying glass) to the right of the search field.

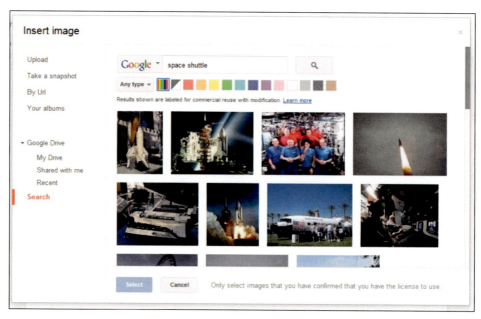

9. Scroll down and find an image of the space shuttle landing (*see below for an example*). Click on it and click the **Select** button at the bottom of the box.

10. At first, the image will be wider than your page. To size it down, do the following:
    a. Click on the image to reveal the sizing handles.
    b. Point your mouse pointer on the upper left corner of the image until the pointer changes to double-arrows at a diagonal.
    c. Click on the upper-left corner sizing handle and drag down and to the right until the image is approximately the size shown above.
    d. Click the i-beam pointer in the left or right margin of your page view to deselect the image.

11. Now, we'll add a fixed image to our document. Here's how:
    a. Add a couple more blank lines at the end of your document by pressing the **Enter** key (**Return** on Macs) a couple of times.
    b. Choose **Image** from the **Insert** menu.
    c. Do an image **search** using the words "International Space Station" and find an image of the ISS.
    d. Choose **Select** to insert the image into your document at the point of the insertion point.
    e. Click on the image and resize it using the sizing handles to about 3 inches wide. *Hint: use the ruler bar as a guide.*
    f. With the image still selected, click on the **Fixed Position** option below the image. The image is now fixed to a position on the page. This also allows you to wrap text around the image. For now, we'll leave the image right where it is.
    g. Click to the right of the image to deselect the image and get your insertion point back.
    h. Set the **font size** to **36** and type "The International Space Station". The text will automatically wrap to the right side of the image (see bottom of this page for an example).
12. Close this document and move it to your class folder in Google Drive.

You are now ready for **Opportunity WP10.**

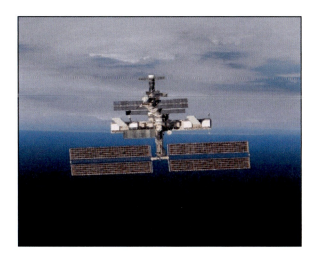

Opportunity WP10

Adding a Graphic Object

Follow the steps below to produce the document as displayed on the next page. The purpose of this assignment is to give you the opportunity to show what you learned from the lesson. If allowed by your teacher, you can refer to the lesson pages to refresh your memory.

In this Opportunity, you are a student running for student body president. Make a sign to promote your candidacy.

1. Log into Google Drive and create a new document from your class folder.
2. **Rename** the document **Opportunity WP10** or a variation as directed by your teacher.
3. Use the guide on the next page as an example to make your election sign. Be sure to use **LARGE FONTS** so it can be seen clearly from a distance. You can choose your own fonts but make sure they are easy to read.
4. Use Google Drive's **image search** feature to find at least two appropriate images to use for your sign. If you have a picture of yourself, you can include that as one of your images.[9] Size and move your images as needed. You can use in-line or fixed images.
5. Be sure to include some reasons for the students to vote for you.
6. Read it completely once more and fix any other spelling or grammar errors you find in the document.
7. Print your final document (or share it as directed by your teacher).
8. Write your assignment header (name, assignment, date, subject, etc.) as directed by your teacher on the back of your sign.
9. Close the document's tab and move it to your class folder.

---

[9] Tip: With your teacher's permission, you can take a picture with a smartphone and upload it to your Google Drive account using either your email account or your teacher's if you have no email access.

George Somers
for
President

More recesses!

Less homework!

I represent YOU!!

Lesson WP11 - Page Settings

While not as full featured as a desktop word processor, Google Docs provides you some control over page settings. This lesson will cover such controls as managing **page margins**, **page breaks** and **headers and footers**. We'll explain each of these features and give you examples of when these commands can be helpful to you.

Page margins refer to the amount of blank area, or "white space", left around the edges of your page. Believe it or not, this "white space" is very important to how your text is presented on the page. Page margins should be balanced, meaning that the top/bottom margins should be equal and the left/right margins should be equal. Some businesses, however, use stationery paper with a pre-printed letterhead at the top of the paper. In this case, you would need to increase the size of your top margin so you wouldn't be printing text over the letterhead.

Sometimes, after typing up your document, you might have a full page of text plus a second page which consists of only one or two lines of text. Whenever possible, you should use settings like page margins to avoid this. Some minor changes with font sizes and paragraph spacing can also help you achieve this goal to keep your document to one page. For example, job résumés should always be kept to one page of text.

We'll also explore the use of **headers** and **footers**. A **header** is any information you want to be printed at the TOP of every page. A **footer** is any text you want to be printed at the BOTTOM of every page. You can see a footer at the bottom of every page in this book which includes the name of this book and the current page number. These are just two pieces of information that you can put in a header or footer. For this book, I had Google Docs put a page number code in the footer which displays whatever the current page number is. Neat, huh?

Finally, **Page breaks** allow you to start a new page before the normal end of the page. This is helpful, for example, if you want to avoid having the first line of a paragraph at the bottom of page 1 and the remaining four lines of the paragraph on the second page. In this case, you could put a page break BEFORE the first line of the paragraph, pushing it to the second page with the rest of the paragraph. We'll explain how to do page breaks as part of this lesson.

Look out! Here comes a manual page break!

See how I did that? I still had room on that page for more text but I decided to start a new page with THIS paragraph. So I put in a page break code. You won't see these formatting codes when you print your document, but they are there.

Now, let's start our tutorial...

1. Open the **Promotion WP4** document you created in Lesson WP4.
2. Make a copy and name it **Promotion WP11**.
3. Go to the **Insert** menu and choose **Header**. A new section appears above your text. The header and the body of your document are separated by a horizontal line.
4. In the header, type your first and last name. Then press **Enter (Return)**.
5. On the second line of the header, type your class name and press **Enter (Return)**.
6. On the third line of the header, type today's date and press **Enter (Return)**.
7. If your instructor wants any additional information in your header, enter it on a fourth line of the header.
8. Delete the greeting line ("Dear Preferred Customer;") and any blank lines below it.
9. Go to the **File** menu and choose **Page Setup.** In box that appears, set the top margin to **2.5**. It should look like the following. Click **OK** when you are done.

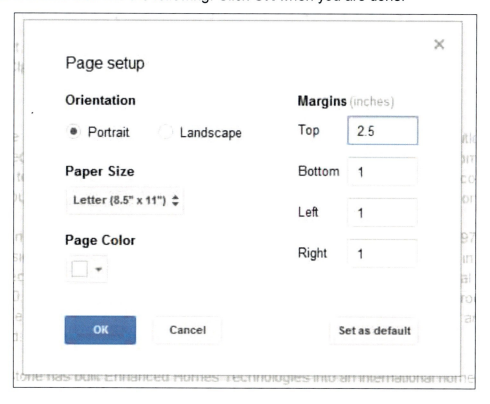

10. Let's add a page number to the footer. Here's how:
    a. Go to the **Insert** menu and point to **Page Number**.
    b. On the sub-menu that pops up, choose **Bottom of page** (see below).
    c. Go to the bottom of the page to see your new footer with a page number.
    d. Press the **Align center** button to center your page number.

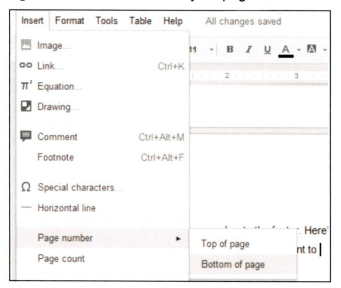

11. Now let's add a **manual page break**. Here's what to do...
    a. Click the I-beam pointer before the third paragraph ("Today, Bart Stone has built...") to put the insertion point before the first word.
    b. In the **Insert** menu, choose **Page Break** (see right).
12. Now scroll to the second page and observe the following:
    a. The header with your name, subject and date.
    b. The page number ("2") at the bottom center of your page in the footer.
13. Close Promotion WP11 and move it to your class folder.

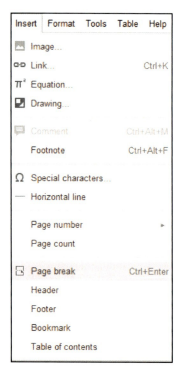

You are now ready for **Opportunity WP11.**

Opportunity WP11

Page Settings

Follow the steps below to produce the document as displayed on the next page. The purpose of this assignment is to give you the opportunity to show what you learned from the lesson. If allowed by your teacher, you can refer to the lesson pages to refresh your memory.

1. Log into Google Drive and **open Opportunity WP1** from your class folder.
2. **Make a copy** and name the document **Opportunity WP11** or a variation as directed by your teacher.
3. Remove any assignment header from your document.
4. Insert a header and type your assignment header (name, assignment, date, subject, etc.) as directed by your teacher.
5. In the **Page Setup** box, set the all page margins to 1.5 inches.
6. Before the paragraph that begins "These e-readers have made...", insert a page break.
7. Insert **a page number** at the bottom of the page (footer) and make it **right aligned**.
8. Check your document against the document as displayed on the next page. They should match.
9. Read it completely once more and fix any other spelling or grammar errors you find in the document. Make sure it matches what is shown on the next page.
10. Print your final document (or share it as directed by your teacher).
11. Close the document's tab and move it to your class folder.

Lesson WP12 - Tables

Google Docs lets you easily add **tables** to any document. Tables are used to organize information into **columns** (up and down) and **rows** (left to right). Where a row and a column intersect is a box called a **cell**.[10] Each cell can be customized with your choice of border thickness (measured in **points**), border color and background color. In this lesson, we'll learn how to add a table, add and remove rows and columns, and customize the border and background colors of the table cells.

row	row	row	row
		cell	

			column
		cell	column
			column
			column

Now that we know some terms to work with tables, let's start our guided tutorial.

---

[10] The terms **columns**, **rows**, and **cells** are also used when working with spreadsheets.

For this tutorial, we're going to add the following table to the bottom of the first page of our **Promotion WP11** document.

Product	Year	Price
Digital Picture Frame	1997	$199.95
Internet Thermostat	2000	$249.95 plus installation
Internet Refrigerator	2005	$2999.95
Internet Microwave	2005	$649.95
Butler Pad (New)	2012	call for quote

1. Open the **Promotion WP11** document you created in Lesson WP11.
2. Make a copy and name it **Promotion WP12**.
3. After the second paragraph on the first page, press **Enter** (**Return**) <u>three times</u> so that we have two blank lines before our table.
4. Go to the **Table** menu and point to **Insert table...**
5. In the box that appears, use your mouse to define a 4 by 5 table and click (see figure at right).

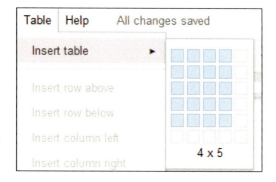

6. You should now have a 4 by 5 cell table which is automatically sized to fit the width of your page.
7. Click in the first cell of the first row and type "Product".
8. Press the **tab** key and enter the text for the first <u>five</u> rows in the remaining cell as shown in the figure on the previous page. **Note**: you will have an extra column and not enough rows. We'll fix that in the following steps.
9. Now let's add a sixth row. Here's how...
    a. Click anywhere in the fifth row of your table to put your insertion point there.
    b. From the **Table** menu, choose **Insert row below** (see figure at right).

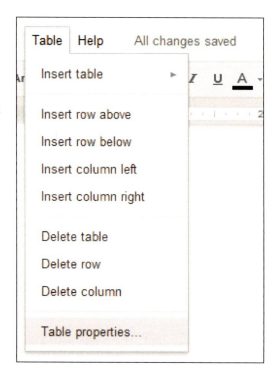

    c. Now click in the first cell of the newly created sixth row and type the remaining text for the sixth row as shown in the figure on the previous page.

    d. **Note:** You could add additional rows and columns by choosing the appropriate item in the Table menu. However, we do not need to add any rows or columns at this time.

10. Let's remove the unnecessary fourth column of our table:

    e. Click anywhere in the fourth column of your table to put the insertion point in a cell of that column.

    f. From the **Table** menu, choose **Delete column**.

    g. **Note:** You can delete other rows and columns by choosing the appropriate item in the Table menu. You can even delete the table. However, we do not need to do any more deleting at this time.

Now, let's have some fun and jazz up our table a bit! We need to make our borders thicker and add some shading to our table. These kinds of changes can make a boring table more interesting and easier to read.

11. Let's thicken up our cell borders.

    a. First, click in any cell in your table.

    b. Go to the **Table** menu and choose **Table properties...**

    c. The Table properties box will appear and look like this:

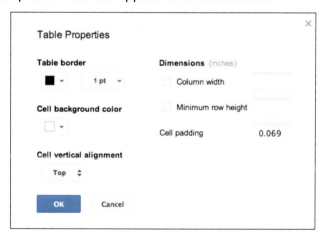

    d. In the **Table border** area, click where it says **1 pt**. This is the size or thickness of the lines.

    e. Set the size of the table border to **1.5 pt** and click the **OK** button.

    f. Your table borders should now display a little thicker.

12. Now let's Make formatting changes to the first row:
    a. Drag-select the first row of the table. The third cell will not appear to be completely selected but it is. It should look like the figure below.

Product	Year	Price
Digital Picture Frame	1997	$199.95
Internet Thermostat	2000	$249.95 plus installation
Internet Refrigerator	2005	$2999.95
Internet Microwave	2005	$649.95
Butler Pad (New)	2012	call for quote

    a. Click the **bold** button to make it bold.
    b. Go to the **Table** menu and choose **Table Properties...**
    c. Choose a light color as the cell background color by clicking the color button and selecting a color.
    d. Click the **OK** button to see how it looks.
13. Making formatting changes to the rest of the table.
    a. Drag select rows 2 through 5 of your table. Again, the last cell will not appear to be completely selected but it is.
    b. Go to the **Table** menu and choose **Table Properties...**
    c. Choose another light color as the cell background color by clicking the color button and selecting a color.
    d. Click the **OK** button to see how it looks.
14. Close **Promotion WP12** and move it to your class folder.

You are now ready for **Opportunity WP12.**

Opportunity WP12

Tables

Follow the steps below to produce the document as displayed on the next page. The purpose of this assignment is to give you the opportunity to show what you learned from the lesson. If allowed by your teacher, you can refer to the lesson pages to refresh your memory.

1. Log into Google Drive and **open Opportunity WP1** from your class folder.
2. **Make a copy** and name the document **Opportunity WP12** or a variation as directed by your teacher.
3. Type your assignment header (name, assignment, date, subject, etc.) as directed by your teacher.
4. After the last sentence of your document, press the enter (return) key two times to add a blank line after the paragraph.
5. Insert a 4-by-4 table and enter the text into the cells according to the table displayed on the next page. Ignore the last column ("iPad") for now.
6. Put the insertion point in any cell in the last column. From the Table menu, insert a column to the right and add the information about the iPad.
7. Add shading to each cell as you feel is appropriate. Make sure that you can read the text against the cell shading (i.e. light against dark).
8. Set your cell borders to **1.5 pt.**
9. Make the text in your first row and the first column **bold.**
10. Check your document against the document as displayed on the next page. They should match.
11. Read it completely once more and fix any other spelling or grammar errors you find in the document. Make sure it matches what is shown on the next page.
12. Print your final document (or share it as directed by your teacher).

"We are the children of a technological age. We have found streamlined ways of doing much of our routine work. Printing is no longer the only way of reproducing books. Reading them, however, has not changed."

It won't be long before heavy school textbooks are replaced with e-readers holding all the information they could ever need in one small device.

	Kindle Touch	Kindle Fire	Nook Color	iPad
Screen Size	6 inches	7 inches	7 inches	9.7 inches
Resolution	600 x 800	1024 x 600	1012 x 600	2048 x 1536
Display Type	E-ink	LCD	LCD	LCD

CONGRATULATIONS!! You have now completed all the word processing lessons and opportunities in this book. That's quite an accomplishment. Now, share your knowledge with others and **KEEP ON LEARNING!**

SPREADSHEETS

GOOGLE SHEETS

What is a Spreadsheet?

Unlike a word processor, which is primarily a tool for working with words, a **spreadsheet** is a computer application primarily designed to work with numbers. While a spreadsheet can work with a variety of types of data, its strength is with calculating numbers and presenting them in a visual format, like in a chart or a graph. In this book, you will learn basic spreadsheet skills which are features of any spreadsheet program.

A spreadsheet document is made up of **columns,** identified by letters, and **rows**, identified by numbers. Where a column and row meet is called a **cell**. Each cell has a name using its column letter and its row number. For example, the cell C6 is in the third column (column "C") and row 6. The active cell is the cell with the highlighted border (see below).

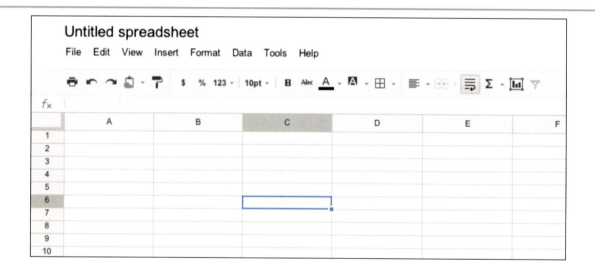

Cells are what hold each piece of data. Each cell can hold a variety of data types, from the numbers of a zip code to the letters of city name. It could even be a street address with letters and numbers (alpha-numeric). Cells can hold dates, phone numbers, assignment grades, you name it! Once a cell stores a piece of data, that data can then be calculated with other data or put on a graph.

In the following lesson, you'll learn to enter, format, and print your data. You'll also learn to turn your data into a chart!

Lesson SS1: Exploring a Spreadsheet

In this lesson, we'll learn how to navigate a spreadsheet document, enter data into cells and print a document. We'll also learn to save your document to your class folder. If you need to review how to save a document, see the section titled "Getting Started" in the front of this book.

Now we will create your first spreadsheet document. You will use this document as the base document for several lessons in this book, so do your best work. At the end of your lesson, your spreadsheet will look like the following:

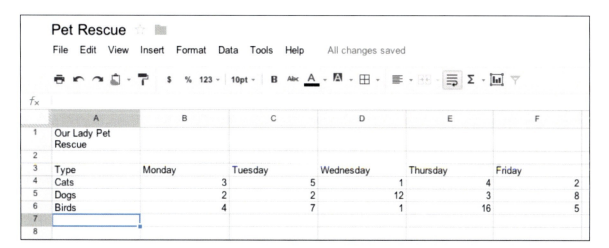

1. In Google Drive, create a new Spreadsheet document by clicking the **New** button and selecting **Google Sheets** from the menu. A new window will open and you will be presented with a new spreadsheet document titled "Untitled spreadsheet".
2. Click on the title (Untitled spreadsheet) and box will appear prompting you for another name for your spreadsheet.

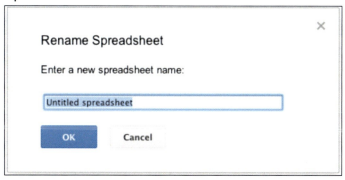

3. For the new spreadsheet name, enter **Pet Rescue**.
4. Notice that there is a thick border around cell A1. That is because it is the active cell.

5. Moving through the spreadsheet: Use the arrow keys on your keyboard to move up, down, left and right through the cells. This is one way to change your active cell.
    a. Now use your mouse to click on different cells, such as C6, B4, F7, G1 and A20. Clicking on a cell is another way to change the active cell.
    b. Click on A1 again to make it the active cell.

Now let's start entering the data for our spreadsheet...

6. With cell A1 active, type **Our Lady Pett Rescue.** Be sure to capitalize as shown. (Note the spelling of the word "Pett")
7. Press the RETURN (or ENTER) key to complete your entry for cell A1 and move to cell B1.
8. You may notice that the text from cell A1 wraps to another line of the cell. That is what happens when the text doesn't fit in the cell. In another lesson, we'll learn how to make cells wider. For now, just leave it as is.

Now, we need to fix the spelling error in cell A1. There are two ways to change the contents of a cell. The first is simply to click on the cell and retype the new contents. The other is to edit part of the contents of the cell using the formula bar (highlighted in red in the figure on the right). That's the method we're going to practice now.

9. Double-click cell A1 to begin editing mode.
10. Click the I-beam mouse pointer just to the right of the second "t" in "Pett" in the formula bar.
11. Use the **Backspace** (or **Delete** on PC) key to remove the second "t".
12. Press the RETURN (or ENTER) key to finish your edit.

Great job! Now, let's continue entering our data.

13. Press the RETURN (or ENTER) key again to move down to cell A3.
14. Using the skills you have learned, enter the data into the cells as shown on the previous page. Make sure to capitalize the words as indicated in the figure.
15. Finally, enter your name in cell F1.

Now we are ready to print. **Printing** is one form of outputting your document on paper using a printer. This is also called a **hardcopy**. We will now learn about the Google Drive's printing options. You may or may not be printing this lesson. Ask your teacher if he/she wants you print it. Regardless, you should complete this lesson to learn about the printing options available to you. At the end of this lesson, you can either print the document or cancel it.

Go to Google Drive's **File** menu and choose **Print**. The print settings window opens and looks like this...[11]

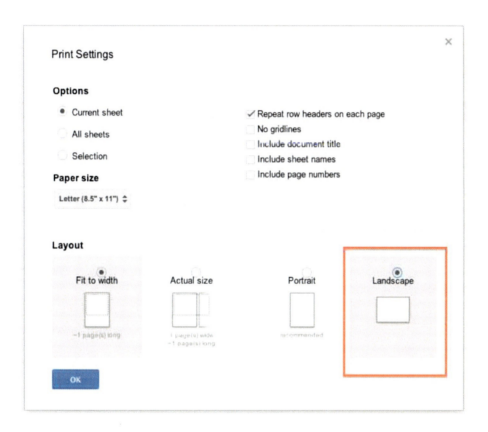

There are two orientations in which you can print your paper -- **Portrait** (up and down) and **Landscape** (wide). Most word processing documents, like a letter or report, are printed in Portrait mode. Other documents, like spreadsheets, work better in Landscape mode. For now, we are going to choose Landscape.

In the Layout section, choose **Landscape** (see red box in figure on previous page). Then, click the **OK** button. A Print dialog box appears. It will look similar to the following.

---

[11] In this book, I use the Google Chrome browser for my illustrations. Other browsers may look different when printing. Google Chrome is available for free from http://google.com/chrome.

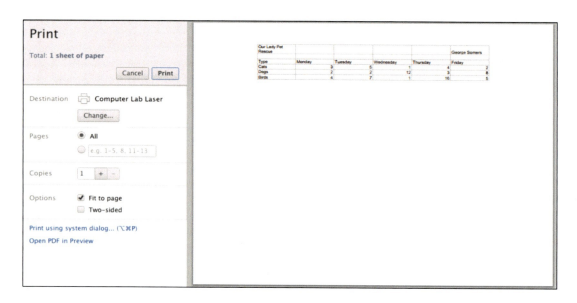

For now, we are not going to make any changes to these settings. Ask your teacher if your settings are correct. If you are asked to print your spreadsheet, click the **Print** button. Otherwise, click the **Cancel** button.

Close the **Pet Rescue** tab and you should be back at the Google Drive page. If you are not there, click the tab named "My Drive - Google Drive" in your browser. If the **Pet Rescue** document is not in your class folder, drag it onto the folder to move it there. We will save all our work in your class folder for better organization and sharing.

You are now ready to proceed to **Opportunity SS1**. We call them "opportunities" because you will have the opportunity to show what you have learned in this lesson.

Opportunity SS1

We are now going to create a new Google Sheets spreadsheet. It is a spreadsheet of hit totals from some of the players from the 2010 San Francisco Giants baseball team.[12] When you are done, it will look like the sample on the next page. Ask your teacher if you need to share and/or print the document.

1. In Google Drive, click on the **New** button and select **Google Sheets** (see at right.)
2. Enter the data shown on the sample on the next page. Make sure all your names and numbers are entered correctly. We will be calculating these numbers in the next few Opportunities.
3. Print and/or share your document as instructed by your teacher.

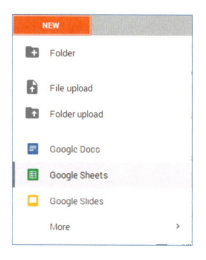

---

[12] While the monthly hit totals are not accurate as represented here, we will be calculating the seasonal totals for these players in the Opportunity SS2. The seasonal totals will be authentic according to sfgiants.com.

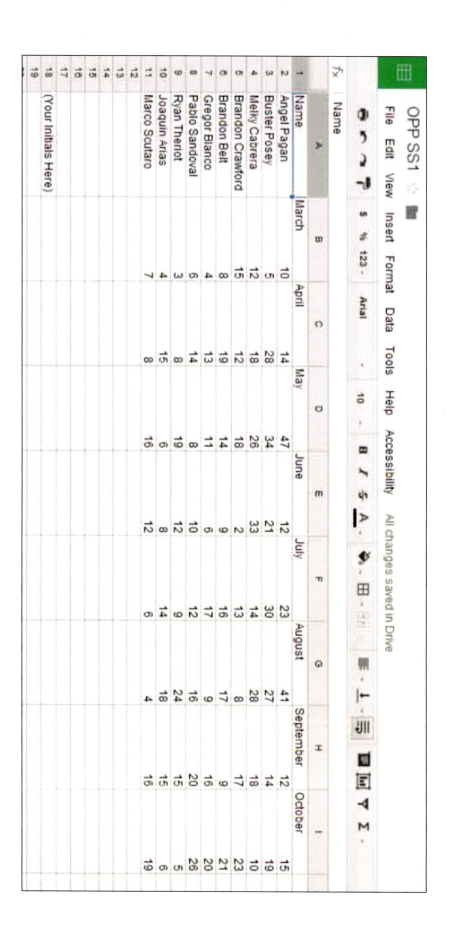

Lesson SS2: Simple Formulas

As we learned in the previous lesson, a spreadsheet is a great tool when working with **numbers**. This numerical data can be calculated in various ways so that the data can be compared and analyzed. Since the numbers are stored the cells in our spreadsheet, we can enter formulas in cells near them and see the results of the calculations.

We'll start by learning about simple formulas. Simple formulas are mathematical expressions similar to those you learn about in math class. You can use the following operators in your formulas:
- **+** for addition
- **-** for subtraction
- ***** for multiplication
- **/** for division

Formulas always begin with "**=**" (the equals sign) so that Google Spreadsheets knows you have entered a formula. You can even use parentheses to force the order of **operations rules. Remember PEMDAS? Please Excuse My Dear Aunt Sally?** Here's an example of a simple formula -- **=2*(6-2)** which results in a value of **8**. What would the result be if there were no parentheses?

Another advantage to using a spreadsheet is that you can substitute **cell names**, also known as **cell references**, into your formulas if the values you want to use are stored in a cell in your spreadsheet. So now, you can have formulas like **=A2*(B3-D3)**. The advantage to using cell names is that if the values in the cells referenced in the formula change, the formula doesn't have to be changed and the spreadsheet will automatically recalculate the result to reflect that change. Many parents use spreadsheets and formulas to work and rework their budgets. By changing the values in their expenses, parents can adjust and control their monthly expenses so that they can save their money for things like a Disneyland vacation or your college fund. You'll see how this works in this lesson.

In addition, there is a special type of formula called a **function**. Functions are pre-programmed formulas, which take a set of cells, calculate them in a certain way, and return the result. These sets of cells are called **cell ranges**. Functions usually have a specified format or syntax they must follow to work properly. The most common function, the SUM function, might be displayed as **=SUM(A1:A100)**. By placing the colon between the first and last cell name in the set, we have referred to the **cell range** of A1 through A100. So **=SUM(A1:A100)** would calculate the sum total of all the cells in that range. This is much easier than **=A1+A2+A3+A4...A100** with every cell referenced individually in a simple formula. You will learn more about the **SUM** function in this lesson.

Normally, when a formula is entered in a cell, Google Spreadsheets displays the result of the formula. It is helpful to be able to see all the formulas in the spreadsheet. To do this, go to the **View** menu and select **All formulas.** Your teacher may ask you to do this in order to check to see if you are putting in the formula, and not simply entering the answer you want to see. This is also a helpful way to check to see if you entered the formula correctly. Of course, the formula for the active cell is always shown in the formula bar, which is located below the button bar.

So, let's get started with formulas!

1. In Google Drive, find your **Pet Rescue** document and open it.

2. From the **File** menu, choose **Make a Copy**. Change the name to "**Pet Rescue Lesson 2**" in the dialog box that appears.

3. In cell B7, enter **=3+2+4** and press the **ENTER (RETURN on Mac) key.**

4. Now change the number in cell B4 to any number of your choice but DO NOT change the formula in B7. Is the total in B7 correct now?

5. Undo that last change to B4 by hitting the **UNDO** button (or Edit>Undo).

6. This time, let's use cell references in our B7 formula. Click on cell B7, type **=B4+B5+B6** and press the **ENTER (RETURN)** key.

7. Repeat step #4 and change the value of B4. Now, what happens to the value displayed in B7? That's because we used cell references, not the current value of the cell.

8. Change one of the values in cell B5 or B6 and to see how the total changes.

9. Let's return all values in B4, B5 and B6 to their original values -- 3, 2 and 4 respectively.

10. Change the formula in B7 to **subtract** any two values in B4:B6. Be sure to use cell references, not the current values of those cells. (Hint: start your formulas with =)

11. Change the formula in B7 to **multiply** any two values from B4, B5 and B6. Be sure to use cell references, not the current values of those cells.

12. Change the formula in B7 to divide any two values in B4:B6. Be sure to use cell references, not the current values of those cells.

13. Change the formula in B7 to include all three cell references in B4:B6 using your choice of operators (+, -, * or /) with two of them within parentheses.

14. Change the formula in B7 one last time to **=SUM(B4:B6).**

15. Let's add the SUM function to cells C7 through F7 to calculate the totals for the rest of the week using a shortcut. Here's how...

    a. Click on cell C7.

    b. Click the **Function** button on the button bar (see below) and select **SUM** from the menu.

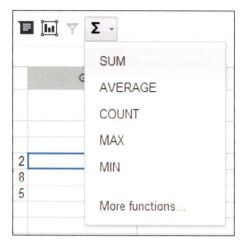

    c. Google Spreadsheets will enter a **=SUM()** into the cell. Enter the range **C4:C6** between the parentheses.

    d. Repeat these steps to enter the **SUM** function for cells D7, E7, and F7.

16. From the **View** menu, select **All formulas** to show your formulas and compare your spreadsheet to the sample on the next page. Select **View>All formulas** again to return to showing the results of the formulas..

Compare your results to the sample on the next page. Follow your teacher's instructions for submitting your work for grading purposes.

Final result of Lesson 2 showing the formulas

	A	B	C	D	E	F
1	Our Lady Pet Rescue					
2						
3	Type	Monday	Tuesday	Wednesday	Thursday	Friday
4	Cats	3	5	1	4	2
5	Dogs	2	2	12	3	8
6	Birds	4	7	1	16	5
7		=SUM(B4:B6)	=SUM(C4:C6)	=SUM(D4:D6)	=SUM(E4:E6)	=SUM(F4:F6)

Final result of Lesson 2 showing the results of the formulas

	A	B	C	D	E	F
1	Our Lady Pet Rescue					
2						
3	Type	Monday	Tuesday	Wednesday	Thursday	Friday
4	Cats	3	5	1	4	2
5	Dogs	2	2	12	3	8
6	Birds	4	7	1	16	5
7		9	14	14	23	15

You are now ready for Opportunity SS2.

Opportunity SS2

1. Open your "**OPP SS1**" spreadsheet in Google Drive.
2. From the File menu, choose, "**Make a Copy**" and name the new file "**OPP SS2**"
3. In cell J1, enter the text "TOTALS".
4. In cell J2, enter a **SUM** function to add up Pagan's totals for March through October.
5. Repeat Step 4 to enter a **SUM** function to add the totals for the remaining players in cells **J3 through J11**.
6. In cell A12, enter the text "Totals".
7. In cell B12, enter a **SUM** function to add the totals for all players for the month of March.
8. Repeat Step 7 to enter a SUM function to add totals for the months April through October.
9. In Cell A16, enter the text "Pagan - Scutaro".
10. In Cell B16, enter the formula to subtract Scutaro's March total from Pagan's March total.
11. Repeat Step 10 to enter similar formulas in cells C16 through I16 for the months March through October.
12. In cell A17, enter the text "Cabrera / Mo. Totals".
13. In similar fashion, enter a formula to do this division calculation for each month in cells B17 through I17.
14. In cell A18, enter the text "Belt * Blanco".
15. In similar fashion, enter a formula to do this multiplication calculation for each month in cells B18 through I18.
16. In cell A19, enter the text "Sandoval + Arias".
17. In similar fashion, enter a formula to do this addition calculation for each month in cells B19 through I19.
18. Check your results against the sample provided on the next page.
19. Go to Google Drive's **View** menu and choose "**All formulas**".
20. Show your computer screen to your teacher for grading purposes.

OPP SS2

File Edit View Insert Format Data Tools Help Accessibility   All changes saved in Drive

	A	B	C	D	E	F	G	H	I	J
1	Name	March	April	May	June	July	August	September	October	TOTALS
2	Angel Pagan	10	14	47	12	23	41	12	15	174
3	Buster Posey	5	28	34	21	30	27	14	19	178
4	Melky Cabrera	12	18	26	33	14	28	18	10	159
5	Brandon Crawford	15	12	18	2	13	8	17	23	108
6	Brandon Belt	8	19	14	9	16	17	9	21	113
7	Gregor Blanco	4	13	11	6	17	9	16	20	96
8	Pablo Sandoval	6	14	8	10	12	16	20	26	112
9	Ryan Theriot	3	8	19	12	9	24	15	5	95
10	Joaquin Arias	4	15	6	8	14	18	15	6	86
11	Marco Scutaro	7	8	16	12	6	4	16	19	88
12	Totals	74	149	199	125	154	192	152	164	
13										
14	(Your Initials Here)									
15										
16	Pagan - Scutaro	3	6	31	0	17	37	-4	-4	
17	Cabrera / Mo. Total	0.162162162162	0.120805369127	0.130653266332	0.264	0.0909090909090	0.14583333333	0.11842105263	0.0609756097	
18	Belt + Blanco	32	247	154	54	272	153	144	420	
19	Sandoval + Arias	10	29	14	18	26	34	35	32	
20										

Lesson SS3: Copy Formulas, Insert Columns and Rows

Calculating numbers is one of a spreadsheet's main strengths. When we use cell references instead of using fixed values, Google Sheets will substitute the cell reference with the values of those cells and calculate them as you desire. The advantage to using cell references is that we can change the cell values involved in those calculations and we don't have to change the formula. Google Sheets will simply grab the current values and recalculate the result accordingly. This can be a great time saver.

Sometimes we need to calculate the values in a series of columns or rows the same way. For example, we might want to total 5 values in each of rows 4, 5 and 6. One way to save ourselves some time is to copy the formula that calculates the total of row 4 and paste it to the corresponding cells in rows 5 and 6. Google Sheets will change all the 4's in the cell reference to 5's and 6's, depending on which row you are totaling (see Area 1 of Figure SS3-1 below).

Figure SS3-1:

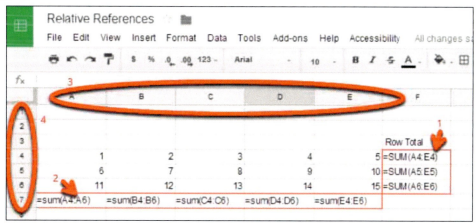

Why does Google Sheets change your cell references of the ranges? Because when we refer to a cell by its column letter and its row number (e.g. A4), we are using a **relative reference**. The formula in cell F4 tells Google Sheets to calculate the sum of the five values to the left of F5. If we were to copy and paste this formula to F5, the row numbers in the formula will change to 5's to reflect the fact that we are totaling the five values in row 5 instead of row 4. In essence, the cell reference is **relative** to the row you are in. This also works for calculating columns of numbers instead of rows. In this case, copying and pasting a formula which calculates a column of numbers means that the column letters in the references must change to work with the new column (see Area 2 of Figure SS3-1).

Figure SS3-2:

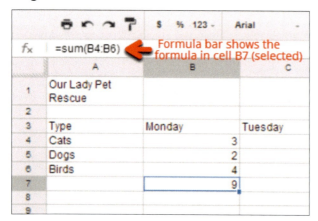

The best way to see how Google Sheets changes your formulas when you copy and paste them to other cells is to tell Google Sheets to show the formulas instead of the results of the calculations. You can also print your spreadsheets with the formulas by showing the formulas before you print. Otherwise, you can select a cell and see the formula in the formula bar (See Figure SS3-2 at left).

There are two ways to show your formulas:
1. Go to Google Drive's View menu and select "All formulas", or...
2. Hold the Control key and press the ` key (to the left of your "1" key in the numbers row of your keyboard).

Inserting Rows and Columns

Sometimes we need a new row or column between existing columns or rows which already have data in them. We don't want to erase these values and type in the new ones. There is a better way. Here's how:

Inserting a New Column

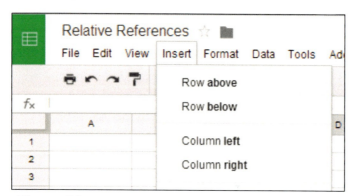

To insert a column, select one of the columns next to the location of the new column you wish to create by clicking its column number in the column header (see Area 3 of Figure SS3-1 on previous page. Doing so selects the entire column. Then simply go to Google Drive's Insert menu and select "Row above" or "Row below" as needed (see Figure SS3-3 above).

Figure SS3-3

Inserting a New Row
To insert a row, select one of the rows next to the location of the new row you wish to create by clicking its row number in the row header (see Area 4 of Figure SS3-1 on previous pages. Doing so selects the entire row. Then simply go to Google Drive's Insert menu and select "Column left" or "Column right" as needed.

We'll get to practice with copying and pasting formulas as well as inserting new rows and columns in the tutorial on the next page.

Deleting Rows and Columns
You can also delete existing rows and columns by selecting the row's number or column letter as before and selecting "Delete row" or "Delete column" from Google Drive's Edit menu.

Now, let's see how we can use these new skills in a spreadsheet. Use the sample on the next page to see the end result.

1. Open your class assignments folder in Google Drive and open the **Pet Rescue** file.
2. Use **File > Make a Copy...** to make a copy of your Pet Rescue file and name it "Pet Rescue Lesson 3".
3. Click on cell B7 and enter **=sum(B4:B6)** to total all the animals rescued on Monday.
4. Now we need to insert a new row 6 (above "Birds" Row). Here's how:
    a. Click on the **6** in the header row.
    b. Go to the **Insert** and select **Row Above.**
    c. A new row will appear above the <u>old</u> row 6.
5. Use the table below to enter new data for spreadsheet in cells A6 through F6.

| Rabbits | 2 | 6 | 3 | 1 | 5 |

6. Question: What happened to "Birds row?
7. Question: What happened to the **formula** in B7? How did it change? Click on cell B7 so you can see the formula in the formula bar.
8. Question: What happened to the **result** in B7? How did it change?
9. We also need to insert a new column between columns A and B. Here's how:
    a. Click on Column A header
    b. Go to the **Insert** and select **Column Right.**
10. Question: What happened to **original** Column B (and all columns to the right of it)?
11. In new B3, enter the word "Totals".
12. In new B4, enter "=sum(c4:g4)".

Now we need to copy this formula from B4 to cells B5, B6 and B7. There are two ways to copy formulas from one cell to another. We'll learn both methods in the next few steps.

13. Using the Copy and Paste commands
    a. Click on Cell B4 with the formula in it.
    b. Go the Google Drive's **Edit** menu and select **Copy**. (You can also use the keyboard shortcut CTLR-C on Windows or CMD-C on a Mac). This will copy the formula to an area of the computer's memory called the clipboard.
    c. Click on B5 and select **Paste** from Google Drive's **Edit** menu. (You can also use the keyboard shortcut CTLR-V on Windows or CMD-V on a Mac). This will copy whatever is in the clipboard, the copied formula in this case, to the selected cell.
    d. Now, click on cell B6 and paste it again.
    e. Finally, click on cell B7 and paste it again.
    f. Each time you paste the formula, the cell references will change to reflect the current row.

Figure SS3-4: The Fill Handle

14. Let's learn a second way to do a copy/paste with only **one action**. We call this the **fill handle** method. Here's how it works:
    a. Click on cell C8 and enter the formula **=sum(C4:C7)** to total all of the animals rescued on Monday.
    b. Point your mouse pointer to the bottom right corner of cell C8. The mouse pointer will change to the cross (see figure). This means you are pointing to the cell's **fill handle**.
    c. Drag that cross pointer from C8 to G8. This will copy the formula to all cells in that range and change the column letters in the cell references according to what column it is in. Go ahead and verify this by clicking on each cell and viewing the formula in the formula bar.

15. Check the results for your spreadsheet against the samples on the next page.
16. Close "Pet Rescue Lesson 3" and save it as directed by your teacher

Lesson SS3 End Result showing results:

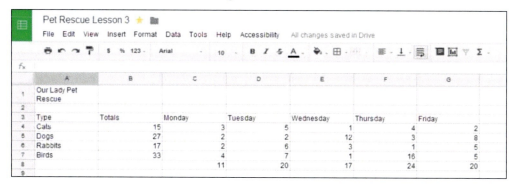

Lesson SS3 End Result showing formulas:

Show your formulas (View>All formulas) and check your spreadsheet against the following sample.

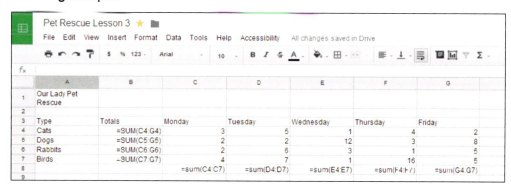

You are now ready for Opportunity SS3.

Opportunity SS3

1. Open your "**OPP SS1**" spreadsheet in Google Drive.
2. From the File menu, choose, "**Make a Copy**" and name the new file "**OPP SS3**"
3. Click on the "A" in the Column Header to select the entire Column A.
4. Insert a new column to the **right**.
5. Click on cell B1 and enter "Totals"
6. Click on the "2" in the Row Header to select all of Row 2.
7. Insert a new row **ABOVE** this row.
8. Click on cell A2 and enter your first and last name.
9. For C2 through J2, manually enter a random integer between 0 and 20 for your monthly hit totals.
10. Click on cell B2 and enter a SUM function to add all of your hits for each month of the season.
11. Use Copy/Paste to copy this formula to cells B3 through B12.
12. Click on cell C13 and enter a SUM function to add all of the hits for March for all players in the spreadsheet.
13. Use the fill handle to copy this formula to cells D13 through J13.
14. Check your results against the sample provided on the next page.
15. Go to Google Drive's **View** menu and choose "**All formulas**" to verify that your formulas are correct.
16. Print and/or share with your teacher as directed for grading purposes.

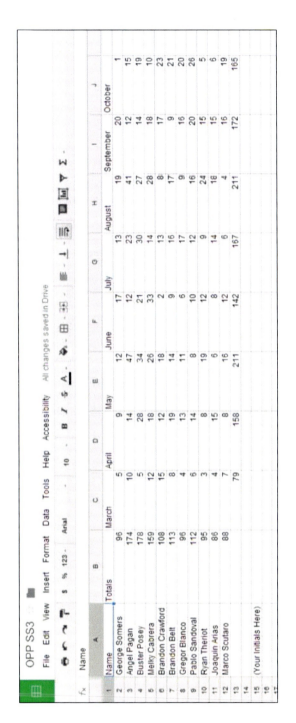
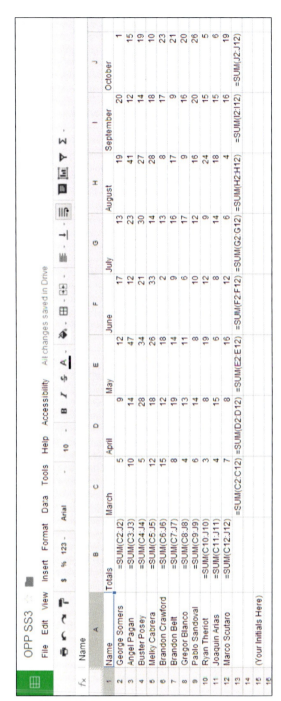

Lesson SS4: MAX, MIN AND AVERAGE FUNCTIONS

In Lessons 1-3, we have covered how to enter text, numbers and simple formulas into a spreadsheet. We also suggested that you use cell references in your formulas whenever a value required in a calculation is stored in a cell. In addition, we learned that you should use a special kind of formula, called a function, for certain purposes, like adding up a range of cells.

But the **SUM** function is only one example of functions provided by Google Sheets. In this lesson we will learn three more functions and their purposes. All are similar in format (also known as syntax as the SUM function except that the first word is changed. The SUM, MAX, MIN and average functions are outlined in the table below.

Function	Value Returned	Example
SUM	The **sum** total of a range of cells	=**SUM**(A4:A6)
MAX	The **highest** value in a range of cells	=**MAX**(A4:A6)
MIN	The **lowest** value in a range of cells	=**MIN**(A4:A6)
AVERAGE	The **average** of a range of cells	=**AVERAGE**(A4:A6)

In this lesson, we'll also learn how to use the **Functions** button ( ) in the toolbar to enter functions with very little typing.

Let's dive in and play with these new functions.

1. Log in to Google Drive and open the original **Pet Rescue** file.
2. Go to Google Drive's **File** menu, select **Make a Copy...** and name the new file **Pet Rescue Lesson 4**.
3. In A7, enter the text "Total".
4. In cell B7 enter the formula "**=sum(b4:b6)**".
5. Using the fill handle method we learned about in Lesson SS3, copy the formula from B7 to cells C7, D7, E7 and F7.
6. In cell A8, enter the text "Highest"
7. Entering a formula using the **Functions** button.
    a. Click on cell B8.
    b. Click on the Functions button (Σ) in the toolbar and select **MAX** from the dropdown menu that appears.
    c. The MAX function will appear in cell B8. However, the range for the function will be missing. Enter **B4:B6** for the range and press **ENTER** (or **RETURN**).
    d. Using the fill handle method we learned about in Lesson SS3, copy the formula from B8 to cells C8, D8, E8 and F8.
8. In cell A9, enter the text "**Lowest**".

9. Repeat the process in step 7 to add the MIN function to cell B9 using the same range and copy it to cells C9, D9, E9 and F9.
10. In cell A10, enter the text "**Average**".
11. Again, repeat the process in step 7 to add the AVERAGE function to cell B10 using the same range and copy it to cells C10, D10, E10 and F10.
12. Check your results and formulas against the samples provided below.

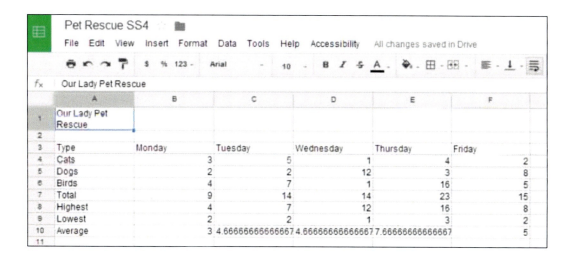

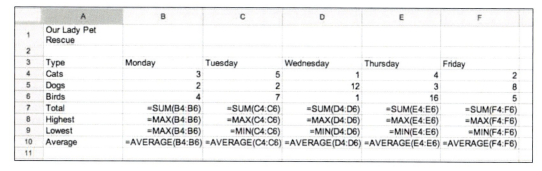

You are now ready for Opportunity SS4.

Opportunity SS4

1. Open your "**OPP SS1**" spreadsheet in Google Drive.
2. From the File menu, choose, "**Make a Copy**" and name the new file "**OPP SS4**"
3. Click on the "12" in the row header to select all of row 12.
4. From the Insert menu choose "Row Above". Repeat this step 3 more times to add 3 more rows. (Note: Your initials should now appear in cell A18.)
5. In Cell A12, type the word "Total".
6. In Cells B12 through I12, enter the **SUM** function to add up the total hits for each month.
7. In Cell A13, type the word "Maximum".
8. In Cells B13 through I13, enter the MAX function to find the highest number of hits for each month.
9. In Cell A14, type the word "Minimum".
10. In Cells B14 through I14, enter the MIN function to find the lowest number of hits for each month.
11. In Cell A15, type the word "Average".
12. In Cells B15 through I15, enter the AVERAGE function to find the average hits for each month.
13. Make cells A12 through A15 (your labels) **bold**.
14. Check your results against the sample provided on the next page.
15. Go to Google Drive's **View** menu and choose "**All formulas**". Again, compare your results with the sample provided on the next page.
16. Show your computer screen to your teacher and submit as directed for grading purposes.

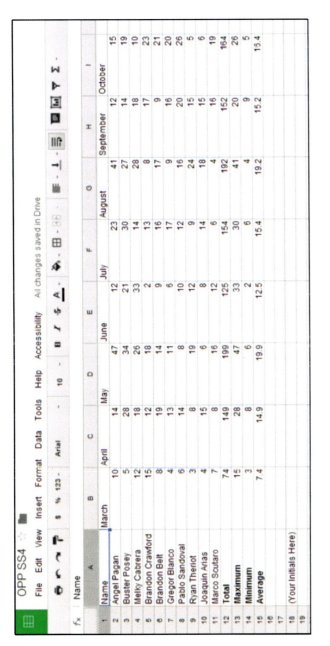

Lesson SS5: Absolute References

In Lesson 3, we learned that formulas using relative references will be altered when they are copied to cells in other columns or rows. Sometimes, this change is desirable. In this lesson, you will learn that sometimes we don't want a cell reference to change. We can prevent these cell references from being changed as we copy the formula to other cells using **Absolute Referencing**.

Absolute references are cell references in which the column letter and/or the row number in the reference are preceded by a dollar sign ($). The dollar sign tells Google Sheets not to change the next letter or number when the formula is copied. It acts like a lock, preventing any changes from that part of the cell reference. If only one part of the cell reference is preceded by a dollar sign ($), only the part of the reference that follows the dollar sign is locked from changes. This is known as a **mixed reference**.

Here are some examples of relative, absolute and mixed cell references:

Type of Reference	Example	Comments
Relative Reference	=A3	If copied, the "A" or the "3" will be changed as needed to reflect the row or column of the cell to which it is copied.
Absolute Reference	=$A$3	If copied, the **neither** the "A" or the "3" can be changed if it is copied to another cell. Both parts of the cell reference are **locked** from changes.
Mixed Reference	=$A3	If copied, only the row number ("3") may be changed if the formula is copied to another row. The column letter is **locked** from changes.
Mixed Reference	=A$3	If copied, only the column letter ("A") may be changed if the formula is copied to another column. The row number is **locked** from changes.

Let's see how absolute references work by following the tutorial below.

1. Log in to Google Drive and open the original **Pet Rescue** file.
2. Go to Google Drive's **File** menu, select **Make a Copy...** and name the new file **Pet Rescue Lesson 5**.
3. In cell A7, enter the text "Total".
4. In cell B7, use the **Function** button (Σ) in the toolbar to enter the SUM function. Use **B4:B6** for your range.
5. Use cell B7's **Fill Handle** to copy the SUM function to cells C7, D7, E7 and F7. You now have a daily total of pets we have rescued.
6. In cell G3, enter the text "Total".
7. In cell G4, use the **Function** button (Σ) in the toolbar to enter the SUM function. Use **B4:F4** for your range.
8. Use the cell G4's **Fill Handle** to copy the SUM function to cells G5, G6, and G7. You now have a total for each animal type rescued and a total of your totals in cell G7.
9. In cell H3, enter the text "Percentage of Total"
10. In cell H4, enter the formula "**=G4/G7**" to calculate the percentage of cats for the week.
11. From the **Format** menu, choose **Numbers>Percentage Rounded** to display the decimal in percentage format.
12. Use the **Fill Handle** to copy the formula from cell H4 to H5 and H6. You will get an error message like the one on the right. THIS IS NORMAL AND EXPECTED. Take a look at the formulas in cells H5 and H6 and see if you can figure out what went wrong. We'll explain it and correct it in the following steps.

Total	Percentage of Total
15	20%
27	#DIV/0!
33	#DIV/0!
75	

13. Let's clear our percentage calculations using the following steps:
    a. Highlight the cell range H4:H6
    b. Clear the cells by choosing **Edit>Delete Values**.
14. In cell H4, enter the formula "**=G4/$G$7**". By doing this we are making an ABSOLUTE reference to G7 so that it will not change when the formula is copied.
15. Once again, use the **Fill Handle** to copy the formula from cell H4 to H5 and H6. The formulas will now show the correct result. Take a look and the formulas in cells H5 and H6. Can you see why?
16. Compare your spreadsheets to the samples on the next page. Make sure your formulas are correct.

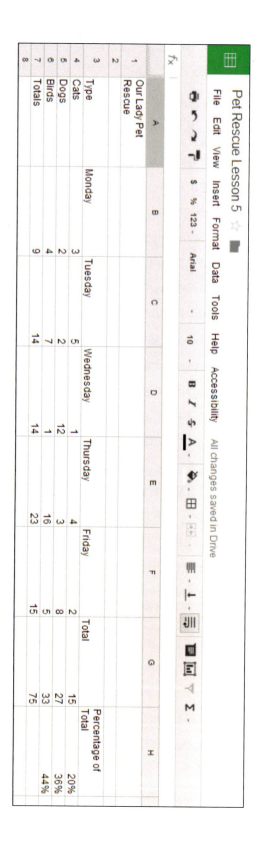

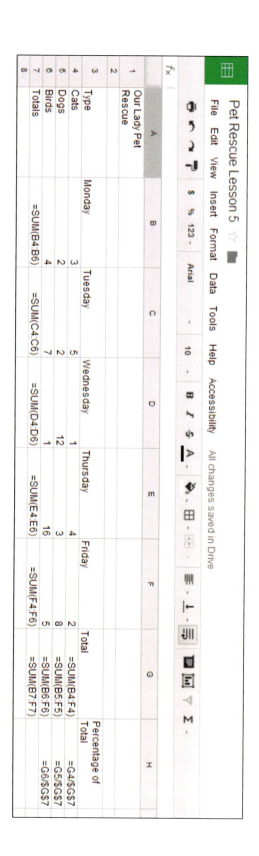

You are now ready for Opportunity SS5.

Opportunity SS5

1. Open your "**OPP SS1**" spreadsheet in Google Drive.
2. From the File menu, choose, "**Make a Copy**" and name the new file "**OPP SS5**".
3. In Cell A12, enter "Total Monthly Hits".
4. In Cell B12, enter a SUM function to add up all of the hits for March.
5. Copy this formula to Cells C12 through I12 using the Fill Handle.
6. In Cell J1, enter "Player Totals"
7. In Cell J2, enter the SUM function to add up all of Angel Pagan's hits for the season (March through October).
8. Copy the formula from cell J2 to J3 through J12. The value in J12 now represents the total of all hits for the season.
9. In Cell K1, enter the text "Percentage of Total".
10. In Cell K2, enter the formula to divide Pagan's total (J2) by the total number of hits by all players for the season (J12). Be sure to use absolute referencing for J12. *Hint: use dollar signs ("$").*
11. Format the result in K2 as a rounded percentage.
12. Copy the formula in K2 to cells K3 through K11 using the fill handle.
13. Check your results against the samples provided on the next page.

Go to Google Drive's **View** menu and choose "**All formulas**". Show your computer screen to your teacher and/or print your spreadsheet for grading purposes.

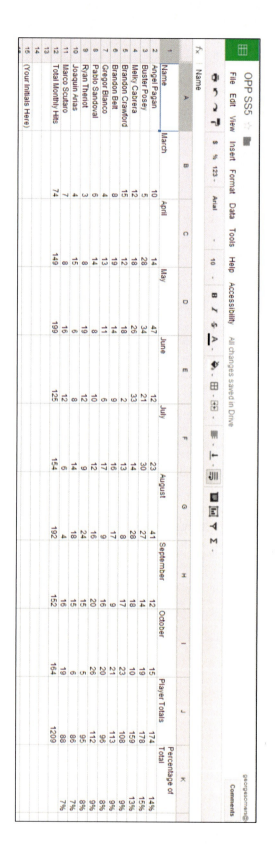

	A	B	C	D	E	F	G	H	I	J	K
1	Name	March	April	May	June	July	August	September	October	Player Totals	Percentage of Total
2	Angel Pagan	10	14	47	12	23	41	12	15	174	14%
3	Buster Posey	5	28	34	21	30	27	14	19	178	15%
4	Melky Cabrera	12	18	26	33	14	28	18	10	159	13%
5	Brandon Crawford	15	12	18	2	13	8	17	23	108	9%
6	Brandon Belt	8	19	14	9	16	17	9	21	113	9%
7	Gregor Blanco	4	13	11	6	17	9	16	20	96	8%
8	Pablo Sandoval	6	14	8	10	12	16	20	26	112	9%
9	Ryan Theriot	3	8	19	12	9	24	15	5	95	8%
10	Joaquin Arias	4	15	6	8	14	18	15	6	86	7%
11	Marco Scutaro	7	8	16	12	6	4	16	19	88	7%
12	Total Monthly Hits	74	149	199	125	154	192	152	164	1209	
13											
14											
15	(Your Initials Here)										

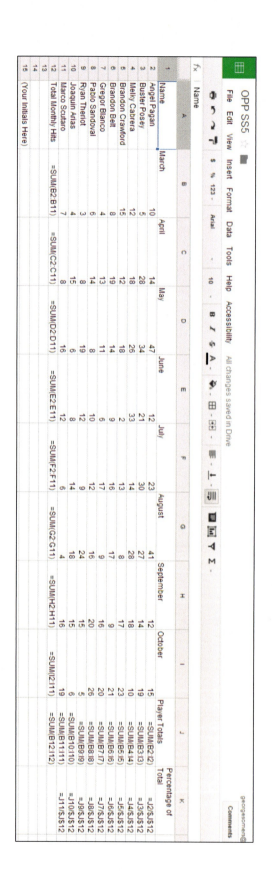

	A	B	C	D	E	F	G	H	I	J	K
1	Name	March	April	May	June	July	August	September	October	Player Totals	Percentage of Total
2	Angel Pagan	10	14	47	12	23	41	12	15	=SUM(B2:I2)	=J2/$J$12
3	Buster Posey	5	28	34	21	30	27	14	19	=SUM(B3:I3)	=J3/$J$12
4	Melky Cabrera	12	18	26	33	14	28	18	10	=SUM(B4:I4)	=J4/$J$12
5	Brandon Crawford	15	12	18	2	13	8	17	23	=SUM(B5:I5)	=J5/$J$12
6	Brandon Belt	8	19	14	9	16	17	9	21	=SUM(B6:I6)	=J6/$J$12
7	Gregor Blanco	4	13	11	6	17	9	16	20	=SUM(B7:I7)	=J7/$J$12
8	Pablo Sandoval	6	14	8	10	12	16	20	26	=SUM(B8:I8)	=J8/$J$12
9	Ryan Theriot	3	8	19	12	9	24	15	5	=SUM(B9:I9)	=J9/$J$12
10	Joaquin Arias	4	15	6	8	14	18	15	6	=SUM(B10:I10)	=J10/$J$12
11	Marco Scutaro	7	8	16	12	6	4	16	19	=SUM(B11:I11)	=J11/$J$12
12	Total Monthly Hits	=SUM(B2:B11)	=SUM(C2:C11)	=SUM(D2:D11)	=SUM(E2:E11)	=SUM(F2:F11)	=SUM(G2:G11)	=SUM(H2:H11)	=SUM(I2:I11)	=SUM(B12:I12)	
13											
14											
15	(Your Initials Here)										

Lesson SS6: Formatting text and cells

The text in your cells can be **formatted** in a number of ways. Just as in Google Docs, you can change the font, font size and font colors. In addition, you can use **font styles** such as bold, and italics. Text can also be aligned to the left, right or center of a cell. By default (normal), text is left aligned in a cell and numbers are right aligned. These changes are made with the same buttons on the button bar as they are in Google Docs and other Google Apps.

Formatting buttons discussed in this lesson: 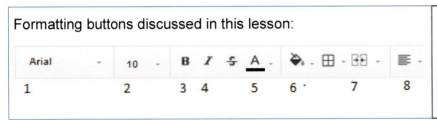	Formatting Buttons (left to right): 1) Font; 2) Font Size; 3) Bold; 4) Italics; 5) Text Color; 6) Fill Color; 7) Merge Cells; 8) Text Alignment

In addition to formatting text, changes can be made to **cell shading**, **width** and **height**. We will learn how text and cell formatting works in this lesson. All these changes can be made on a cell by cell basis or applied to multiple cells at once. Some of these formatting buttons have options available under them. We will explore these options in our tutorial.

Tip: When making changes to text color and fill color (i.e. shading), make sure you have a good level of contrast between the text and the cell background to ensure the text can be easily read. For example, if you have a dark colored font, make your background a light color. If you have a light colored font, make sure your background color is dark.

Sometimes, you need multiple cells to act like one cell. This is called **merging cells**. By selecting the cells you wish to merge and clicking on the merge button (#8 in the figure above), you can merge more than one cell into one. You will see how this can be helpful when we do our tutorial later in this lesson.

Cell widths and heights and be adjusted manually using your mouse. To adjust a column width, point your mouse to the **separator line** (see figure at right) between the columns in the column header and drag the separator line to where you want it to be. In similar fashion, you can go to the separator line between the rows in the row header and drag them until you are happy with them.

Columns can also be adjusted automatically using a feature called **auto-fit**. If you double-click the separator line between columns in the column header, the column width will automatically be adjusted to fit the longest value in that column.

Let's see how these formatting changes work together with this tutorial.

1. Log in to Google Drive and open the original **Pet Rescue** file.
2. Go to Google Drive's **File** menu, select **Make a Copy...** and name the new file **Pet Rescue Lesson 6**.
3. Click on Cell A1 and Change to **Trebuchet** font with a **24** point size.
4. Select cells A1 through F1 and click the **Merge Cells** button to merge them into one cell and reveal the entire title.
5. **Center** align new Cell A1.

6. Use the fill color tool to make the fill color for Cell A1 a dark color of your choice (see figure at left).
7. Use the text color tool to make the text color for Cell A1 a light color of your choice.
8. Select cells A3 through A6 and make them **bold**.
9. Select cells B3 through F3 and make them **bold** and **centered**. Then increase **the font size** to 14.
10. Resize column A to make it a little wider than the longest item in column A. To do this, point to the vertical separator line on the border between A and B in the Column Header and drag your mouse to the left until it is only as wide as it needs to be and still display all text in column A.
11. You can have Google Sheets size your columns automatically too. It's a feature called **auto-fit** and here is how you do it:
    a. Go to the column header and double-click the separator line between Column B and C to auto-fit width.
    b. Repeat this step to auto-size columns C through F.
12. Now let's make columns B through F the same width. To do this,

a. Go to column header and drag-select from column B through F until they are selected.
b. Drag the column border (in the heading) between column B and C and drag slightly to the right to resize column width for selected columns.

13. Increase row height of row A by dragging the row separator between rows A and B in the row header down about a quarter-inch.

14. Highlight cells A4 through F4 and change color to a color of your choice using the **text color button** on the toolbar (see figure at right). Repeat for cells A5:F5 and A6:F6.

15. Your spreadsheet should now look similar to the sample below.

You are now ready for Opportunity SS6 on the next page.

Opportunity SS6

Format Text, adjust column width and row height, merge cells, align text in cell

1. Open your "**OPP SS1**" spreadsheet in Google Drive.
2. From the File menu, choose, "**Make a Copy**" and name the new file "**OPP SS6**".
3. Use **Insert > Row Above** to insert a row above Row 1.
4. **Merge** cells A1 through I1 and **center align** the text in the new cell A1.
5. In the new A1, enter the text "SF Giants Hits 2012".
6. Make the font for cell A1 **Verdana**, size 24, bold.
7. Increase row **height** for cell A1 to match sample.
8. Change the **Fill Color** of Cell A1 to Orange.
9. Adjust the **width** of columns B through I to match sample.
10. Make **bold** and **center** the text in cells B2 through I2.
11. Make cells B2 through I2 have white text and black fill.
12. Make cells A3 through A12 have white text and black fill. Make the text in these cells bold.
13. Highlight B4 through I4 and fill these colors "gray" (RGB 204, 204, 204) which is in row 1, column 6 of the color palette. Repeat this step for B6:I6, B8:I8, B10:I10 and B12:I12 to match the sample on the next page.
14. Compare your spreadsheet to the sample on the next page.
15. Print your spreadsheet in landscape orientation using the no gridlines option. (Note: ask your teacher for permission to print in color.)
16. Submit your spreadsheet for grading purposes according to your teacher's instructions.

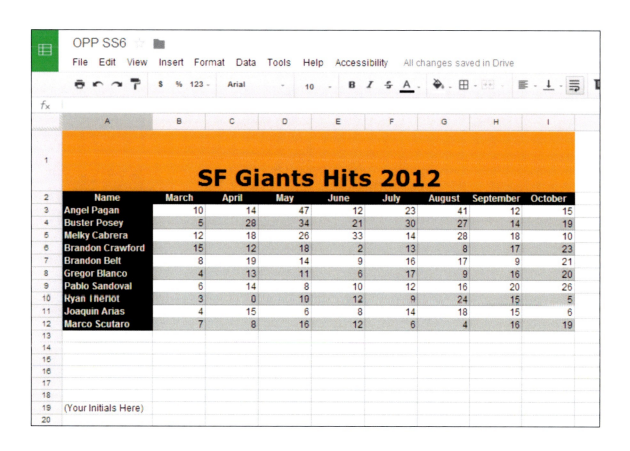

Lesson SS7: Borders, Conditional Formatting, Hide Gridlines

In this lesson, we will build on the formatting tricks we explored in the previous lesson by learning about cell **borders** and the **conditional formatting** features of Google Sheets. We will also learn how to hide the gridlines for viewing and printing purposes.

Every cell can have a top border, bottom border, left border, right border or any combination of the four borders. Here are some examples:

Borders can be turned on and off using the **borders button** on the toolbar. In addition to turning borders on and off, you can also decide what color your borders can be and what line style you want. The figures below show you the **line color** options and **line style** options available by clicking the borders button.

Border Line Color Options   **Border Line Style Options**

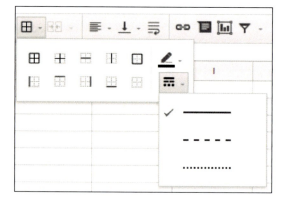

You can also have Google Sheets make **formatting changes** if the value of the cells meets a certain criteria. These kinds of changes are known as **conditional formatting**. Conditional formatting changes such as text color and fill color will be made if the condition you define is met. If the value of the cell changes and the condition is no longer met, the cell formatting will go back to normal. In this lesson's tutorial, you will learn how to define the conditions under which changes will be automatically made and which formatting changes will be made if that condition is met.

Once you have made formatting changes such as these, you may wish hide your gridlines so you can better see how all these changes look. To turn off the gridlines on your screen, simply go to Google Drive's **View** menu and select **Gridlines**. This will toggle this setting on or off. You even have the option to print your spreadsheet with or without the gridlines. Look for the checkbox in your print options dialog box to do this.

Now, let's play with borders and conditional formatting in a spreadsheet in the following tutorial.

1. Open the original "**Pet Rescue**" file.
2. **Make a copy** and name it "Pet Rescue Lesson 7"
3. Merge A1:F1 and **center** align the text.
4. Make font size of new cell A1 size **36**.
5. Change font color for cell A1 to a color of your choosing.
6. Change fill color for cell A1 to a color of your choosing (using Fill Color button). Make sure that font and fill colors contrast so you can read the text.
7. Select the **outer border** option from the Borders button.
8. From the **Border** button, select the border color of your choice.
9. Select cells A3:F3 (i.e. your headings) and set the outer border to a color of your choosing.
10. Select cells A4:F4 (i.e. the "Cats" row), choose the **dashed outside border** in a color of your choosing.
11. Select cells A5:F5 (i.e. the "Dogs" row), choose **solid bottom border** in a color of your choosing.
12. Now let's try some **Conditional Formatting**:
    a. Select cells B4:F6.
    b. Go to **Format** menu and choose **Conditional Formatting**.

c. Make a rule to change the background of any value **greater than** 7 to orange. (see figure below). You can also set the rule to change the text color if you wish. Click **Save rules** when you are done setting your conditional formatting options.

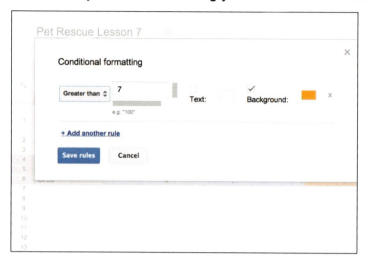

d. Now change a few of at least two of the numbers in your cells and see how their formatting changes as they meet (or don't meet) the condition you set.

13. Go to **View > Gridlines** to turn **off** your gridlines on the screen.
14. Compare your spreadsheet with the sample below.
15. In Print options, check box for "no gridlines" but cancel before printing if your teacher does not want you to print.

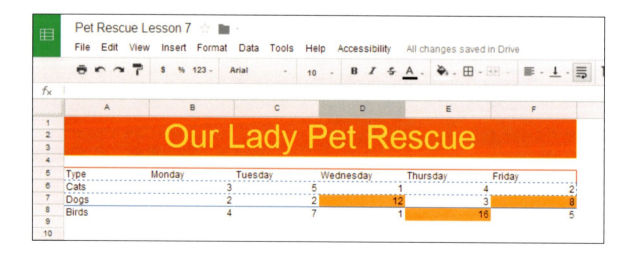

Opportunity SS7

Borders, Shading, Conditional Formatting

1. Create a new spreadsheet document using the **NEW** in Google Drive.
2. **Rename** the document "OPP SS7".
3. In cell A1, enter the text "The Islands of Hawai'i"(without the quotation marks).
4. In cell A2, enter the text "Hawai'ian Island Tourism" (without the quotation marks).
5. **Merge** cells A1:F1 and make the alignment **centered**.
6. **Merge** cells A2:F2 and make the alignment **centered**.
7. Change the **font size** of the new A1 size **24 point**.
8. Change the **font size** of the new A2 size **14 point**.
9. Select A1:A2 and do the following:
    a. Add an **OUTER** border in a style/color of your choosing.
    b. Shade using a **fill color** of your choice.
    c. Change **font color** to a color of your choice. *Hint: make sure the font color and the fill color contrast so that you can read the text.*
10. Enter the remaining text according to the sample provided on the next page.
11. Select A4:F4, make the font **bold** and apply a **solid BOTTOM border**.
12. Select A5:A10, make the font **bold** and apply a **solid RIGHT border**.
13. Select A4:F10 and apply a **solid OUTER border**.
14. Select B4:B10 and apply a **dashed right border**. Repeat this step for cells C4:C10, D4:D10, and E4:E10.
15. Select B5:B10 ("Area" column) and create a **conditional formatting rule** to change the background color and/or font color to a color of your choosing **if the value is greater than 700**. *Hint: Conditional formatting is found in the Format menu.*
16. Select C5:C10 ("Population" column) and create a **conditional formatting rule** to change the background color and/or font color to a color of your choosing **if the value is less than 10000**.
17. Select E5:E10 ("Average Stay" column) and create a **conditional formatting rule** to change the background color and/or font color to a color of your choosing **if the value is between 5 and 7**.
18. Have your teacher check your conditional formatting rules.
19. Compare your spreadsheet to the sample on the next page.
20. Print your finished spreadsheet using the **no gridlines** option and/or submit as directed for grading purposes.

The Islands of Hawai'i
Hawai'ian Island Tourism

Island	Area (sq. mi)	Population (2010)	Visitors (2003)	Average Stay (Days)	Nickname
Hawai'i	4028	185079	1207164	5.3	The Big Island
Maui	727.2	144444	2125421	7.33	The Valley Isle
O'ahu	596.7	953207	4090483	6.85	The Gathering Place
Kaua'i	552.3	66921	975867	6.67	The Garden Isle
Moloka'i	260	7345	94106	3.67	The Friendly Isle
Lana'i	140.5	3135	91445	3.41	The Pineapple Isle

(Your Initials Here)

Lesson SS8: Formulas using Dates

To a computer, a date is just a number. We can express a date in a number of formats but to a computer, it is just another way to say the same number. Just as 178.00, 178, and $178 are still the same number shown three different ways, there are a number of formats for the same date. Here are just a few:
- June 5, 2014
- 6/5/2014
- 6/5/14
- 5 June 2014

You will find all the available formats for dates, including dates with times, listed under **Format > Number > More Formats > Custom Date and Time Formats** in Google Drive.

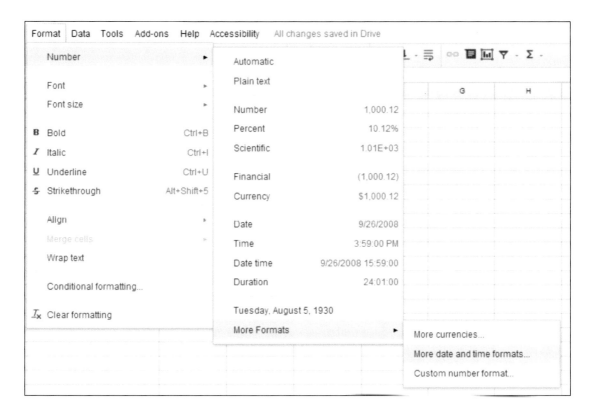

Google Drive considers December 31, 1899 as "Day 1". January 1, 1900 is "Day 2", January 2, 1900 is "Day 3" and so on. Because a day is simply a number, you can use dates in calculations to count the days since a certain date or find out how many days there are until your birthday or any other significant date.

Google Drive even has a special built-in function that will return today's date. It's called the **TODAY function** and it looks like **=TODAY()**. Notice that, unlike the SUM, MIN, MAX and AVERAGE functions we have learned about so far, the format for this function does not require any information between the parentheses. Simply type that function into a cell as is and Google

Drive will return the current date. Also, the TODAY function automatically updates to whatever date you are using the spreadsheet.

To do calculations based on dates, simply use them in a subtraction formula. For example, to find out how many days since you were born, simply enter a formula that looks like this:
- =TODAY() – [Your birthdate]

Of course, you will need to enter your birthdate instead of **[Your birthdate]** in the formula shown above.

You can also find out how many days there are until a special day (e.g. the last day the school year) by entering a formula like the following:
- = [Last day of school] – TODAY()

The possibilities are endless. You can also do time calculations. Let's try some formulas using dates and times in this lesson's tutorial.

1. In Google Drive, create a new spreadsheet file and **rename** it "Dates Lesson SS8".
2. In Cell A1, manually type in today's date using the format shown in the sample on the next page.
3. Widen Columns A and B to match sample at the end of this tutorial.
4. First, let's enter the following into cells A1:B7 (see figure at right). We'll format them in a variety of ways in the next few steps.

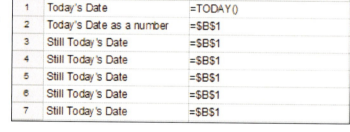

   a. Click on Cell B2 and go **to Format > Number > Number**. The Date will now display as a number with two decimal places.
   b. Click the **Decrease Decimal Places** button on the toolbar TWICE to display the number without decimals.

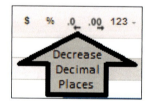

c. We'll format the rest of the dates in a variety of formats. For cells B3 through B7 do the following.
   i. Click on each cell.
   ii. Go to **Format > Number > More Formats > Custom Date and Time Formats.**

5. Now let's find out how many days there are until Christmas using the figure at the right!

9	Today's Date	=TODAY()
10	Christmas this year	12/25/2014
11	Days until Christmas	=B10-B9

   a. Enter the data you see at the right beginning in Cell A9. Make sure to change the year in cell B10 to the current year.
   b. Cell A11 will now display the number of days until Christmas this year.

6. We'll use cells A13:B15 to calculate how many days there are until your birthday.

13	Today's Date	=today()
14	My next birthday	8/31/2014
15	Days until my birthday	=B14-B13

   a. Enter the data you see in the figure at the right but put in the date of your **next birthday** in cell B14.
   b. Cell B15 will now display the number of days until your next birthday. Is it coming soon?

7. We can also do calculations of time. Using the figure at the right as a guide, do the following:

18	The Time Now	9:10 AM
19	Time School Ends	2:30 PM
20	Time until the End of School	=B19-B18

   a. In cell B18, enter the current time. Be sure to use the HOUR:MINUTES <space> AM/PM format.
   b. In cell B19, enter the time when school ends today using the same format as in step 7A.
   c. Cell B20 will now display the hours and minutes until school is out. Then, the rest of your day begins.

8. The reason we can do date calculations is because a date is just a number to the computer. To prove it, enter the following in cells D1:F4. Format cell E2 as a number with no decimal places, just as you did in

D	E	F
Day 1	12/31/1899	
Number for date	=E1	
I am	=today()-8/31/1974	days old

   steps 4A and 4B of this tutorial. In cell E4, use your birthdate (in the year you were born) for the second part of the equation.

Nice job! You are a date pro! You are now ready for Opportunity SS8.

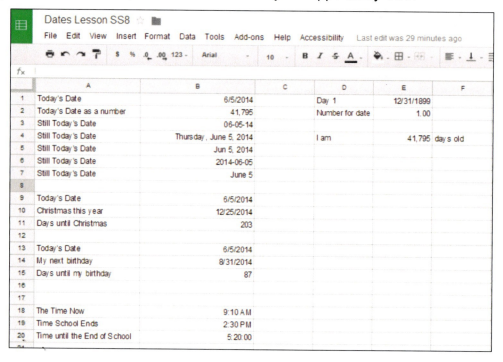

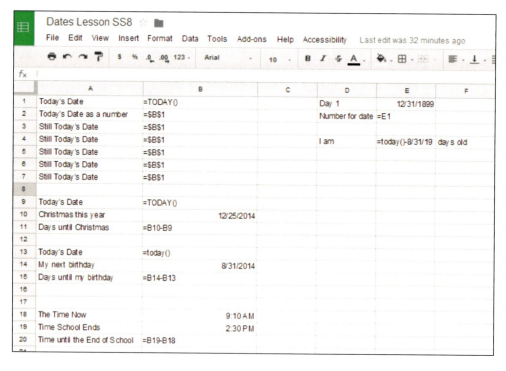

You are now ready for Opportunity SS8.

Opportunity SS8

1. Create a new spreadsheet in Google Drive and rename it "**OPP SS8**".
2. Using the guide on the next page, enter in the requested information shown, including the prompts in cell A1, A12 and A13.
3. In row 4, enter your information as indicated. Format all dates using the format shown.
4. In rows 5 through 9, enter the names and information for 5 of your friends.
5. In cells E4:E9 enter today's date using the **TODAY** function.
6. In cells F4:F9, calculate how many days old each person is using a subtraction formula.
7. Enter the data shown in rows 15 through 22 of the sample on the next page. Do an Internet search for each person's birth and death dates and use the **TODAY** function to calculate how many days they lived. Format the "days old" with no decimal places.
8. Google Drive uses August 5, 1930 as its example for date formats. But what is the significance of that day? *(Hint: it's a famous person's birth or death date.)* Do an Internet search to find out. When you find out, enter the missing information in row 22 and complete the table. Format the "days lived" with no decimal places.
9. Enter your initials in cell A24.
10. Compare you spreadsheet to the sample on the next page. Note: your "TODAY" value and the "days old" totals in column F will differ from the sample.
11. Print and/or submit your spreadsheet to your teacher as directed for grading purposes.

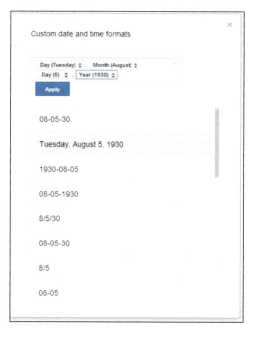

	A	B	C	D	E	F	G
1	Who is the oldest? You or one of your friends?						
2							
3	Description	First Name	Last Name	Birthdate	Today	Days Old	
4	Me	George	Somers	August 31, 1974	July 2, 2014	14550	
5	Friend 1	Joe	Smith	July 13, 1974	July 2, 2014	14599	
6	Friend 2	Henrietta	Calzadillas	September 10, 1974	July 2, 2014	14540	
7	Friend 3	Judy	Blackburn	July 12, 1974	July 2, 2014	14600	
8	Friend 4	Blache	Pedrozo	June 1, 1974	July 2, 2014	14641	
9	Friend 5	Greggory	Bliss	July 11, 1974	July 2, 2014	14601	
10							
11							
12	Who Lived Longer?						
13	Find their birth and death dates on the Internet and calculate how many days they lived.						
14							
15	First Name	Last Name	Birth Date	Death Date	Days Lived		
16	George	Washington					
17	Albert	Einstein					
18	John	Lennon					
19	Robert E.	Lee					
20	Wolfgang A.	Mozart					
21	Steve	Jobs					
22			August 5, 1930				
23							
24	(Your initials here)						

Lesson SS9: Data Sort

In this lesson, we will learn how you can **sort** data in your spreadsheet. Sorting means to re-order your data in a certain way. The best way, for example, to list the artists in your music library is alphabetically by last name. That way you can easily find the artist you are looking for. If you are looking for a specific song in your library, you could sort the tracks in your library alphabetically by song. When you sort a list alphabetically (A-Z), that is called **ascending order**. You can also sort numerical data. For example, if you want to find the shortest track in your music library, you could sort them from shortest to longest. This would be considered **ascending order** by track time.

In addition you can sort a list in **descending order**. Descending order means reverse-alphabetical order (i.e. Z-A) for text and highest to lowest if you are sorting numbers. Sorting in descending order is helpful to find out which of your classmates can do the most pull-ups or who sold the most Girl Scout cookies in your troop. The highest values would then be at the top of the list and the lowest values at the bottom.

In a list of data, you have a choice as to how to order your list. It all depends upon your **sort criteria**. For example, if you sort a list of people by last name, then "last name" is your sort criteria. Each column in your spreadsheet is a criteria on which you can sort.

You can also sort on multiple columns or criteria at the same time. The first column the computer considers is the **primary sort criteria**. The second column it would consider is the **secondary sort criteria**. For example, if a school wants to sort its students alphabetically but wants to group the students within their grade level, the administrative assistant could use the "grade level" column as the primary sort criteria and the "last name" column as the secondary sort criteria.

TIP: It is import when doing your sorts to first select ALL the data that could be affected by that sort. Simply selecting the "last name" column and then running the sort, for example, would result in only the last names being sorted but the rest of your data would be left alone. The result is that everyone in your list gets someone else's last name and none of the other data would get re-ordered in the list. Instead, select the whole cell range and run your sort using the "last name" column as your sort criteria.

To discover how sorts work, do the tutorial on the next page.

Let's get sorting!

1. Open the original "**Pet Rescue**" file.
2. **Make a copy** and name it "Pet Rescue Lesson 9".
3. Doing your first sort:
    a. Select cells A4:F6.
    b. Go to **Data > Sort range….**
    c. Match settings in the figure at the right and click the **Sort button** to sort these cells in ascending order by Column A. The range is now sorted alphabetically by animal.

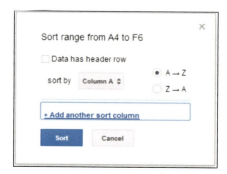

4. Repeat step 3 but select the "Z-A" option to sort the animals in descending order. *Hint: Be sure to select range A4:F6 before doing your sort.*
5. Repeat step 3 again but select the "A-Z" option to sort Column F in **ascending** order.
6. Do your sort again but this time sort Column F in **descending** order.
7. Let's try using two sort criteria. This time when you do the sort, click on "Add another sort column" and match the figure at the right. This will sort your range first in descending order by Wednesday's totals, then sort in ascending order by animal name. Now look at your birds and cats. Since they have the same value on Wednesday, they are sorted alphabetically by animal name.

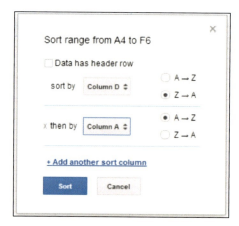

8. Compare your results to the sort order below. You are now ready for Opportunity SS9.

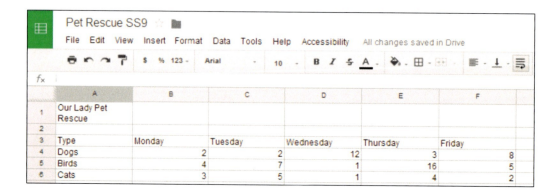

Opportunity SS9

1. Open your "**OPP SS8**" spreadsheet in Google Drive.
2. From the File menu, choose, "**Make a Copy**" and name the new file "**OPP SS9**".
3. Select cells B3:F9 and copy/paste them to cells H3:L9.
4. Similarly, select cells A15:A22 and copy/paste them to cells H15:L22.
5. Select cells A4:F9 and sort them by "days old" in descending order.
6. Select cells H4:L9 and sort them by "last name" is ascending order.
7. Select cells A16:A22 and sort them by "days lived" in ascending order.
8. In cells H23:L23, add the data for Martha Washington. Do an internet search for her birth and death dates, then calculate how many days she lived in cell L23.
9. Select cells H16:L23 and sort them by "last name" in ascending order AND first name in **ascending** order. (Hint: you will need to "add another sort column" to your sort.)
10. Compare your spreadsheet to the sample on the next page.
    a. Format all dates as shown in the sample.
    b. Widen all columns as necessary to fit all data in each column.
    c. Note: your "days old" totals in columns F and L may differ from the sample.
11. Print and/or submit to your teacher as directed for grading purposes.

OPP SS9

	A	B	C	D	E	F	G	H	I	J	K	L
1	Who is the oldest? You or one of your friends?											
2												
3	Description	First Name	Last Name	Birthdate	Today	Days Old		First Name	Last Name	Birthdate	Today	Days Old
4	Friend 4	Blache	Pedrozo	June 1, 1974	June 6, 2014	14615		Judy	Blackburn	July 12, 1974	June 6, 2014	14574
5	Friend 5	Gregory	Bliss	July 11, 1974	June 6, 2014	14575		Gregory	Bliss	July 11, 1974	June 6, 2014	14575
6	Friend 3	Judy	Blackburn	July 12, 1974	June 6, 2014	14574		Henrietta	Calzadillas	September 10, 1974	June 6, 2014	14514
7	Friend 1	Joe	Smith	July 13, 1974	June 6, 2014	14573		Blache	Pedrozo	June 1, 1974	June 6, 2014	14615
8	Me	George	Somers	August 31, 1974	June 6, 2014	14524		Joe	Smith	July 13, 1974	June 6, 2014	14573
9	Friend 2	Henrietta	Calzadillas	September 10, 1974	June 6, 2014	14514		George	Somers	August 31, 1974	June 6, 2014	14524
10												
11												
12	Who Lived Longer?											
13	Find their birth and death dates on the Internet and calculate how many days they lived.											
14												
15	First Name	Last Name	Birth Date	Death Date	Days Lived			First Name	Last Name	Birth Date	Death Date	Days Lived
16	Wolfgang A.	Mozart	January 27, 1756	December 5, 1791	13096			George	Washington	February 22, 1732	December 14, 1799	24767
17	John	Lennon	October 9, 1940	December 8, 1980	14670			Albert	Einstein	March 14, 1879	April 18, 1955	27793
18	Steve	Jobs	February 24, 1955	October 5, 2011	20677			John	Lennon	October 9, 1940	December 8, 1980	14670
19	Robert E.	Lee	January 19, 1807	October 12, 1870	23277			Robert E.	Lee	January 19, 1807	October 12, 1870	23277
20	George	Washington	February 22, 1732	December 14, 1799	24767			Wolfgang A.	Mozart	January 27, 1756	December 5, 1791	13096
21	Albert	Einstein	March 14, 1879	April 18, 1955	27793			Steve	Jobs	February 24, 1955	October 5, 2011	20677
22	Neil	Armstrong	August 5, 1930	August 25, 2012	29971			Neil	Armstrong	August 5, 1930	August 25, 2012	29971
23								Martha	Washington	June 2, 1731	May 22, 1802	25921
24	(Your initials here)											

Google Drive Essentials, George Somers

Lesson SS10: Create a Chart (Same Worksheet)

"A picture is worth a thousand words." ~ Early 20th Century Adage

With Google Sheets, you can easily turn your spreadsheet data into a picture. By using charts and graphs, you can bring your spreadsheet data to life! Charts allow you to see trends and visually see numbers in a way that is sometimes difficult by staring at a bunch of numbers on the screen. In this lesson, we will learn how to make simple, but powerful charts from your spreadsheet data.

Before making a chart, you should first decide which type of chart will reveal the "story" of your data the best. Some charts reveal patterns while others can bring to light aspects of your data you didn't see by simply looking at the numbers. For example, a pie graph is good for showing each value as part of a whole. As such, they are great for showing percentages. You can experiment with the different types of charts and see which chart is best for your situation.

There are all kinds of charts – line charts, pie graphs, column graphs, pattern charts, maps and much more. Each can be customized in a variety of ways. From the title, to the legend, to the labels and even the colors of your data points; all of the part of the chart (see figure below) can be modified and stylized to your liking. We'll go through the basic steps in this lesson.

PARTS OF A CHART

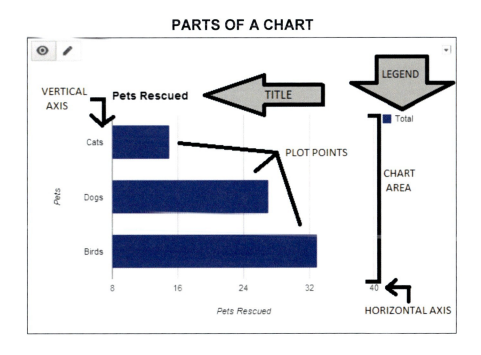

Google Drive Essentials, George Somers

TIP: It is important to select ALL of the data that will be included in your chart first. This includes any category labels that you need along with the data. If more than one **series** (or set) of data is to be included in your chart, make sure all the data points in the series are selected along with their corresponding category labels. In our Pet Rescue spreadsheet, for example, each of our animal categories has a data point for each day of the week. The group of data points (i.e. Monday through Friday) for each animal is a **series** for that category.

Another great aspect about charts is that they are dynamic. That is, if the values they are charting are changed, the values in your graph will be updated automatically. There is no need to delete the graph and create a new one.

Are you ready to see what your data can reveal to you? Let's dive in.

1. Open the original "**Pet Rescue**" file.
2. **Make a copy** and name it "Pet Rescue Lesson 10".
3. Select Column A and **Insert** a new column to the <u>right</u>.
4. In the new Column B you just created, do the following:
    a. In cell B3, enter the text "Total".
    b. In cells B4 through B6, enter a SUM function to add up the weekly total for each animal [e.g. =SUM(C4:G4)].
5. Let's start by making a pie chart!
6. Select cells A4:B6. These are the labels and values we will need for our chart.
7. From the **Insert** menu in Google Sheets, select **Chart**. A dialog box called the **Chart Editor** will appear (see figure at right).

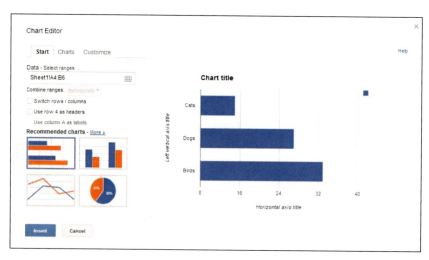

Google Drive Essentials, George Somers   136

8. In this editor, we can customize our chart using the three tabs – **Start**, **Charts**, and **Customize** -- at the top of the window. Here's how:
    a. Select the **Pie Chart** under the recommended charts area.
    b. Click the **Charts** tab at the top of the editor.
    c. Select the **3D Pie Chart** option on that window.
    d. Click on **Customize** and do the following on the screen:
        i. Change the Chart Title to "Pets Rescued" (see below).

        ii. Scroll down the window until you see the **Series** options and do the following:
        iii. Click the **Insert** button at the bottom of the Chart Editor to insert the pie chart into the spreadsheet.
9. Move the chart:
    a. Click on the chart.
    b. Point your mouse pointer to the top border of the chart box and drag it down until the chart no longer covers rows 1 through 6 of the spreadsheet.
10. Now, let's take the same data and make a bar chart.
    a. Select cells A4:B6 again.
    b. Go to **Insert** > **Chart**.
    c. In the Chart Editor, click the **Customize** tab at the top of the window.
    d. As before, change the title to "Pets Rescued".
    e. Scroll down in the editor to the **Axis** section and name the **Horizontal Axis** "Number of Animals" (see below).

f. Change the Axis by clicking "Horizontal" and selecting "Left vertical". Name it "Animal Type" (see figure at right).

g. Click the **Insert** button to place the chart in your spreadsheet.
h. Move the chart so it doesn't cover rows 1 through 6 of your spreadsheet.
i. Your spreadsheet should now look like the figure below.

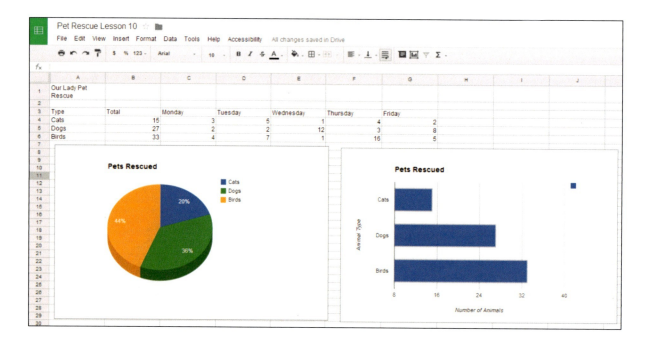

Great job! You are now ready for Opportunity SS10.

Opportunity SS10

1. Open your "**OPP SS7**" spreadsheet in Google Drive.
2. From the File menu, choose, "Make a Copy" and name the new file "OPP SS10".
3. Select cells A4:B10 and go to **Insert > Chart**.
4. Make a chart using the figures below as a guide.

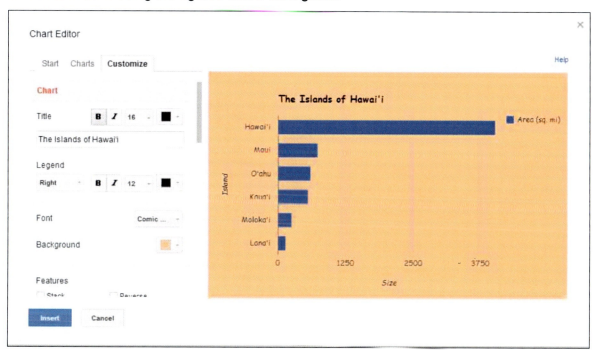

5. Move your chart to the right side of your spreadsheet so that it does not cover columns A through F.
6. Print and/or submit to your teacher per instructions for grading purposes.

Lesson SS11: Create a Chart (On Its Own Worksheet)

In the last lesson, we learned how to embed a chart right next to your data. But did you know that your spreadsheet file has more than just one page in it? Spreadsheet files are really more like **workbooks** with each page of the workbook being able to display not only data but a chart all by itself. These pages are known as **worksheets**. In this lesson, we'll delve a little deeper into customizing charts and learn how to put them on a separate sheet in your spreadsheet. We'll also learn a little more about formatting numbers in your spreadsheet.

1. Log in to Google Drive and create a new spreadsheet.
2. **Rename** the file "Lesson SS11".
3. Enter the data for Columns A and B using the figure to the right.

	A	B
1	Young Adult Income Comparison	
2	Soure: http://nces.ed.gov/	
3		
4		
5	Level of Education	Average Income (2012)
6	Master's Degree or higher	$59,600
7	Bachelor's Degree	$46,900
8	Associates Degree	$35,700
9	H.S. Diplloma or HSE	$30,000
10	Less than H.S. Completion	$22,900

4. Now let's format your numbers in Column B:
   A. Select cells B6:B10.
   B. Use the Currency ($) button in on the toolbar (see right) to format the numbers as currency. This will precede the number with a dollar sign ($) and add two decimal places.
   C. Click the **Decrease decimal places button** <u>twice</u> to remove the decimal places.

NUMBER FORMAT BUTTONS

5. In cell C5, enter the text "Increase over no HS".
6. In cell C6, enter the formula **"=B6/$B$10 - 1"**. This will calculate the increase in salary above a person who has not completed high school or High School Equivalent (H.S.E).
   A. Do you remember what the dollar signs do in this equation?
   B. Do you know why we need the "**- 1**" in the equation?
7. Use the **fill handle** in cell C6 to copy this formula to cells C7, C8 and C9.
8. Use the **Percentages** button in the figure above (%) to format cells C6:C10 as percentages.
9. Select cells A5:B10.

Google Drive Essentials, George Somers

10. Using the figures below as a guide, make the column graph using the settings shown and click the **Insert** button when you are done. The new graph will be placed in your spreadsheet.

11. Set your title, axis options and colors using the figures below.

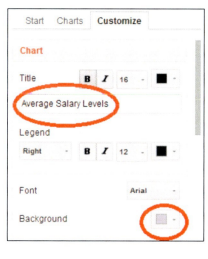

12. In the upper right corner of the chart, locate the menu button (▼) and select "**Move to own sheet…**". (see figure at right)

13. At this point, you have two sheets (or worksheets) in your spreadsheet. It will look like this in the bottom left corner of your screen.

14. Let's rename these sheets to give them more meaningful names.

    A. Click on the down-arrow on the "Sheet1" tab, choose "**Rename**", name the tab "Average Salaries" and press the ENTER (RETURN) key.

    B. Click on the down-arrow on the "Chart1" tab, choose "**Rename**", name the tab "Average Salaries" and press the ENTER (RETURN) key.

15. Now click on the "Salary Chart" tab and view your chart. If you need to adjust any settings, click the "**Advanced edit...**" button to open the Chart Editor and make the necessary changes.

Nice job! You are now ready for Opportunity SS11.

Opportunity SS11

1. Open your "**OPP SS1**" spreadsheet in Google Drive.
2. From the File menu, choose, "**Make a Copy**" and name the new file "**OPP SS11**"
3. In Cell J1, enter the text "Average" and in cells J2 through J11 enter the AVERAGE function to calculate the average of each player's hits. Format the averages to display 2 decimal places.
4. Select cells A1:I4 and make a chart to match all the options in the Chart Editor shown below. Make the new chart its own sheet. Rename the sheet "Hits Chart".

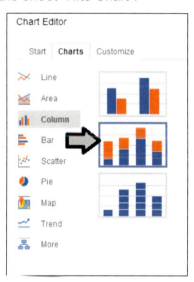

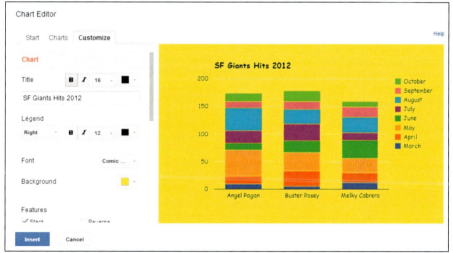

5. Rename the first sheet "SF Giants Hits".

Lesson SS12: Using a Form to Collect Data in a Spreadsheet

Google Forms are a great way to gather information from anyone with an internet connection. They are great for behavior surveys, polls, quizzes and data gathering. Plus, the responses of anyone who completes the form can be sent automatically to a Google Spreadsheet. Once there, you can process the data, create charts, and format the spreadsheet like any other spreadsheet. You can even decide when you will accept responses. Schools who use Google Apps for Education can even specify that people have a school Google address to submit a response.

There are many types of questions you can include in a form. Some question types, like "**multiple choice**" and "**choose from a list**", require a single answer. Others, such as "**checkboxes**", allow multiple responses. You can specify whether each question requires a response on a question-by-question basis. The figure below shows the options for a new question.

When designing a form, there are a few things you should consider. First, who is your audience? Remember, anyone with an internet connection can respond to your survey, unless you lock the responses to students at your school. Also, do not ask people to share personally identifiable information such as their last name, address, or social security number. People don't like it when others ask for information they don't need to have. Only require a response to a question if you absolutely MUST have that information.

Let's build a form in Google Forms

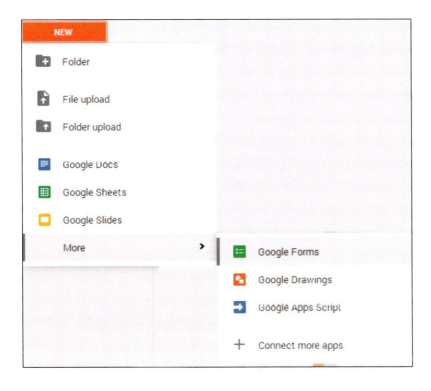

1. Log in to Google Drive, click the **New** button, select **More** and choose **Google Forms**.
2. Title your Form "When I Was Born", select the **Birthday Balloons** Theme and click the OK button.
3. Enter the following text for your form description at the top of the screen.

    A brief survey about YOU. You should ACE this one! Thank you for your time. ~ Our Lady of Mercy School, Merced, CA

4. Use the figure below to enter your first question. It is a "text" question. Click the **Done** button when you are done with the question.

Let's try a "multiple choice" question. Click the **Add Item** button and use the figure below to create the question. Click the **Done** button when you are done with the question.

5. Let's add another question. This time, let's try a "list" question. Match the figure below. Click the **Done** button when you are done with the question.

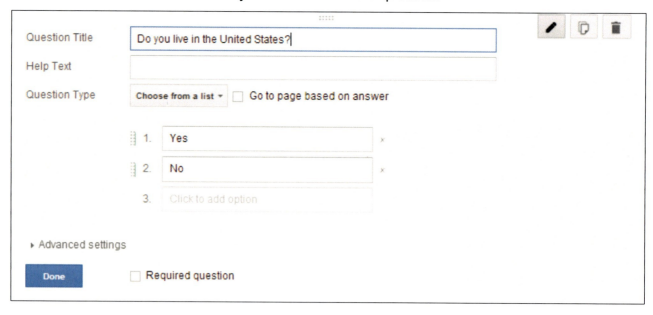

6. Let's create two more "text" questions. Click the **Done** button when you are done with each question. For the "help text" on the first one, enter:

Please enter the two letter abbreviation for your state. (Leave blank if you live outside the U.S.)

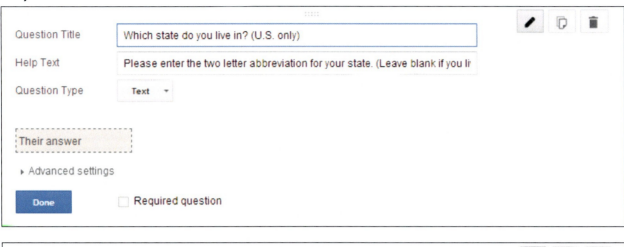

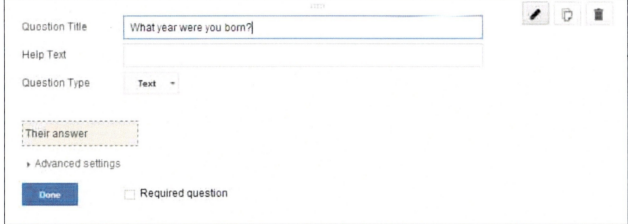

7. Here's another list question for you. For the "help text", enter the following:

Did you know: Some African tribes split into "families" according to the day of the week on which they were born. The "families" support each other. Do an internet search on your birthday and find out what day you were born.

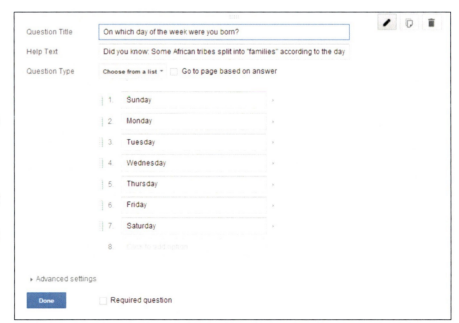

Google Drive Essentials, George Somers

8. Here's a "**Paragraph text**" response question. Paragraph text responses allow for a longer answer than a regular text response. For the help text, enter: **Do an Internet search and list something interesting that happened the year you were born.**

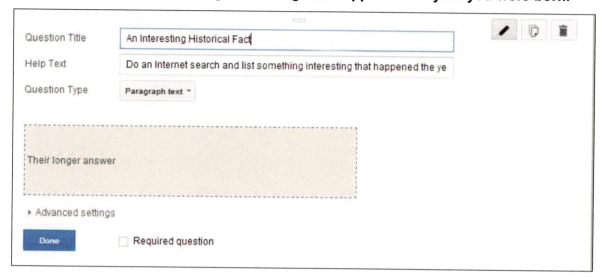

9. The next two questions are "scale" responses. Be sure to set the minimum value for the scale at "0" (zero) and the maximum value at "10" (ten) for both questions.

10. On the toolbar, click the "Choose Response Destination" to create a spreadsheet for the responses. The spreadsheet will be called "When I Was Born (Responses)". Just click OK on the dialog box that appears to accept the default settings. The survey is now accepting responses.
11. Now click the "**View Live Form**" button on the toolbar and take the survey yourself to test it. Hit the "**Submit**" button when you are done with all your responses.
12. Open the **When I Was Born (Responses)** spreadsheet and see your response in the first row.

You are now ready for Opportunity SS12.

Opportunity SS12

1. Create a form to match the figures below. Use the "Books Classics" theme.
2. Designate a spreadsheet to send the results to and take the survey once to test it.
3. Optional: Have your teacher share the survey over social media and/or e-mail.

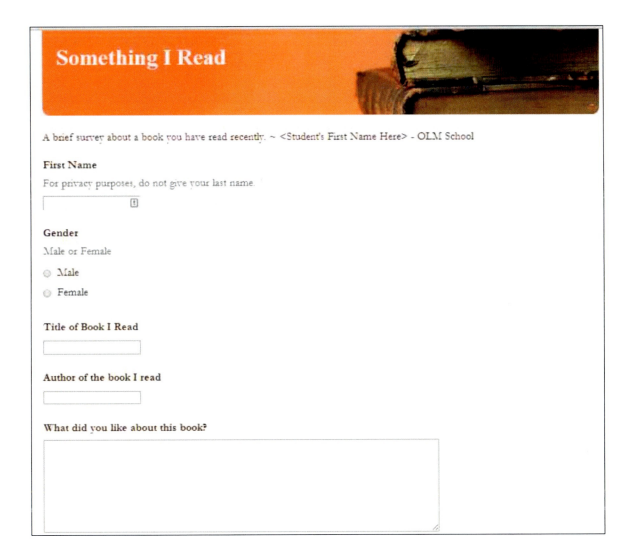

See the second half of the survey on the next page.

What was your favorite part of this book?

Rate this book

    1 2 3 4 5

Terrible ○ ○ ○ ○ ○ Awesome

This book was ...
- ○ Fiction
- ○ Non-Fiction

Would you recommend this book to someone else?

[dropdown ▼]

[Submit]

Never submit passwords through Google Forms.

PRESENTATIONS

GOOGLE SLIDES

What is a Google Slides?

Google Slides is a presentation tool which allows you to create slides which combine text, images, animation, transitions and video so you can effectively deliver your message. Slides can be displayed full-screen as a slideshow or printed as handouts. Handouts can be printed with or without speaker notes to aid in your presentation.

Creating a Google Slides presentation begins by choosing a **theme** (see below).

Themes are a combination of fonts, colors and bulleted list styles which look good together. Each theme includes a collection of slide **layouts** you can choose from. Layouts include **placeholders** to reserve a place for your text or graphic content. The first slide is always a title slide. New slides use the "Title and Body" layout by default (normal) but other layouts are available. Themes and layouts can be changed at any time.

Take a look at the figure below to get acquainted with the Google Slides screen.

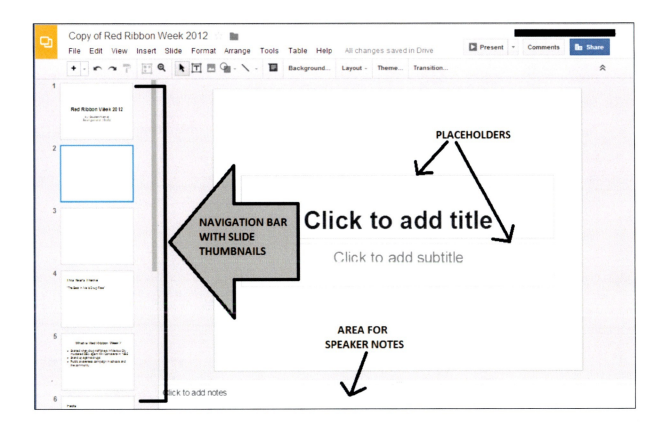

Formatting text in Google Slides is very similar to Google Docs. However, presenters typically want their text on the slides to be short phrases with each line starting with a **bullet** (•). However, Google Slides does not assume you want bullets as some other presentation tools do. To turn on your **bulleted list**, simply click the Bulleted List button on the tool bar. Every time you press the ENTER key (RETURN on Mac), you will get a new line starting with a bullet. To turn off bulleted lists, click the bulleted list button again.

So let's get started with our first Google Slides Presentation.

Lesson SL1: Red Ribbon Week Presentation

1. Log in to drive.google.com.
2. Create a new presentation by clicking the **New** button and choosing **Google Slides**.
3. Select a theme of your choice. The sample uses "Simple Light" but you can choose a different one.
4. Click on the name of your presentation (in the upper left corner), change it to **Red Ribbon Week** and then click **OK**.
5. Click on **title text placeholder box** and enter the title of your presentation.

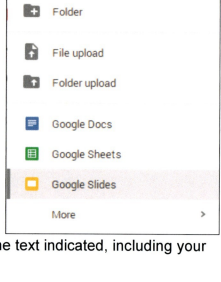

6. Click on the **sub-title placeholder box** and enter the text indicated, including your name and class information.
7. Click the **new slide button** (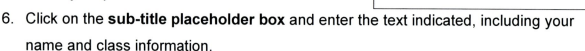) in the upper left corner of your screen to add a new slide with "Title and Body" layout. *(This is the default layout for a new slide.)*
8. Enter the text for slide 2 according to the sample provided on the next page. Slide numbers are for instructional purposes only. You do not need to include them.
9. Repeat steps 7 and 8 to create slides 3 through 6. Turn on bullets as needed using the **bulleted list** button on the toolbar.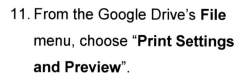
11. From the Google Drive's **File** menu, choose "**Print Settings and Preview**".
12. Click the button that says: "1 slide without notes" and change it to "Handout - 6 slides per page". (*see right*)
13. Click the print button to **Print** this view or submit it to your teacher as instructed for grading purposes.

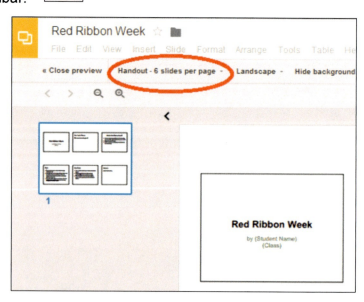

Google Drive Essentials, George Somers

Red Ribbon Week Sample:

Red Ribbon Week

by (Student Name)
(Class)

This Year's Theme

"The Best in Me is Drug Free"

Slide # 2

What is Red Ribbon Week?

- Started when drug traffickers in Mexico City murdered DEA agent Kiki Camarena in 1985
- Stand up against drugs!
- Public awareness campaign in schools and the community.

Slide # 3

Facts

- The median age at which children begin drinking is 12.
- Young people who begin drinking before age 15 are four times more likely to develop alcohol dependence than those who begin drinking at age 21.
- The more often children eat dinner with their families, the less likely they are to smoke, drink, or use illegal drugs.

Slide # 4

More Facts

- Over 3 million U.S. teens abuse prescription drugs.
- Every day, 3,300 more children begin experimenting with prescription drugs.
- 70% of children who abuse prescription drugs admit to getting them from family or friends.

Slide # 5

Source:

http://redribbon.org

Slide # 6

Opportunity SL1

10. Log in to Google Slides and create a new **Google Slides presentation**.
11. Select a theme of your choice. The sample uses "Simple Light" but you can choose a different one.
12. Using the sample on this page and the next page, create this 8-slide presentation.
13. Notes:
    a. Slide 1 uses the default **Title** layout.
    b. Slide 3 uses the **Title and Two Columns** layout. Click the down-arrow on the new slide button, and select **Title and Two Columns** layout.
    c. All other slides use the default **Title and Body** layout.
    d. Slide numbers are not required. They are for instructional purposes only.
14. Submit to your teacher for grading purposes as directed by your teacher.

How Computers Work

<Your Name>
<Class>

Slide #1

Four Functions of a Computer

- INPUT data (information)
- PROCESS data (information)
- STORE data (information)
- OUTPUT data

Slide #2

Hardware Devices

INPUT
- Keyboards
- Mice
- Scanners

OUTPUT
- Monitors
- Printers
- Fax Machines

Slide #3

Both INPUT and OUTPUT

- Multifunction Printers (print, scan, fax, copy)
- Modems (for getting on the Internet)
- Touch Screens
- Touchpads (Laptops)
- Storage Devices

Slide #4

PROCESSING Data

- Data is retrieved from storage
- Inputted data is sent to Central Processing Unit (CPU) for calculations and process
- Processed data is sent to output and storage devices as required

How Storage is Measured

- Bits (1's and 0's)
- 8 bits = 1 Byte (example: "11001011")
- 1 Kilobyte (KB) = 1000 Bytes (approximate)
- 1 Megabyte (MB) = 1000 KB's (approximate)
- 1 Gigabyte = 1000 MB's (approximate)
- 1 Terabyte = 1000 GB's (approximate)

Storage Devices

- CD-ROM's (800 MB capacity)
- USB Flash Drives (2GB-16GB)
- Blu-ray Disk (25-50 GB)
- Internal and External Hard Drives (300 MB's - 1+ TB)

Storage Examples

- A page of text is about 20-50 KBs
- Music tracks are about 3 MB's
- Camera photos are generally 1-5 MB's
- Videos are generally 10-20 MB's per minute
- Full length movies are generally 1-2 GB's

Lesson SL2: Spell Check, Duplicate, Reorder and Delete Slides

In this lesson, you will learn how **Spell Check** works in Google Slides. You will also learn tricks to manage your presentation as you discover how to **duplicate**, **reorder** and **delete** slides.

Spell Check:

When you are doing a presentation, one way to show your audience that you know what you are doing is to spell your words correctly. Of course, Google will flag unknown words which are not found in its dictionary by putting a red dotted underline beneath it. This tells you that you either spelled the word incorrectly or that the word is not in the dictionary. You may find, for example, that your last name is not in the dictionary. Of course, your name IS spelled correctly but it is not in Google's list of words. At this point you can have Google Slides correct it, ignore it or add it to the dictionary. See Lesson WP3 to learn how spell check works in Google Apps.

Duplicate Slides:

If you need to create a slide which is similar to another slide, you can simply duplicate that slide and edit the copy of the slide as needed. Duplicating slides will save you a lot of time. Here's how to duplicate a slide:

1. First select the slide you want to duplicate in the navigation pane on the left of your screen.
2. Duplicate the slide one of two ways:
    a. Go to the Google Slide's **Edit** menu and select **Duplicate**, or…
    b. Right-click (control-click on Mac's with one button mice) the slide and choose **Duplicate Slide** from the menu that appears.

Reordering Slides:

As you get closer to completing the process of creating your slides, you may find that it would be better if the slides were in a different order. You want your slides to have a logical progression that makes sense to your audience. To reorder slides, simply drag the slides up or down in the navigation pane on the left side of your screen. As you drag your slide, you will see a horizontal line appear. When that line is between the slides you want to move it to, just let go of the mouse button to end your drag and place the slide there.

In addition to the drag-and-drop method, you can do all of the following from the **Slides** menu:
- Move slide up
- Move slide down
- Move slide to beginning
- Move slide to end

Deleting Slides:

It is important that your slides be efficient in communicating your message to your audience. For example, you may decide to combine content which is on two slides into one slide. Or maybe you made a slide and you no longer need it. To **delete** a slide, do the following:
1. First select the slide you want to delete in the navigation pane on the left of your screen.
2. Delete the slide one of two ways:
    a. Go to the Google Slide's **Edit** menu and select **Delete**, or…
    b. Right-click (control-click on Mac's with one button mice) the slide and choose **Delete Slide** from the menu that appears.

Let's try out these new commands:

1. Log in to Google Drive and open your **Red Ribbon Week** presentation.
2. Make a copy of Red Ribbon Week and name it "**Red Ribbon Week Lesson 2**"
3. **Duplicate** Slide 3 ("What is Red Ribbon Week?") *(Hint: Right-click and choose **Duplicate**.)*
4. Let's practice with Spell Check on the new slide copy.
    a. Add an extra "f" in the word "traffickers".
    b. Right-click (Control-click for 1-button Mac mice) the "traffickers" and choose correct spelling from menu that appears.
    c. Browse to your other slides to check for other misspelled words. If you find any, fix any that need to be fixed.
5. You can also **Add to Dictionary** when the word is actually spelled right. Here's how.
    a. Go to first slide.
    b. Is your last name marked with red dotted underline? If so, right-click (control-click for 1 button Mac mice) on it and choose **Add to Dictionary**. *If it isn't, change it to "Baumgartener" or some other name that's probably not found in a common dictionary. Then add it to the dictionary.* Google Drive will no longer tell you this word is spelled incorrectly.
5. Using drag-and-drop, rearrange the order of your slides but keep the title slide in the first position.
6. **Delete** a couple slides of your choosing using the right-click method or from the **Slides** menu.

Nice work! You are now ready for Opportunity SL2.

Opportunity SL2

1. Create a new Presentation in Google Drive.
2. Select the "Biz" Theme.
3. Change the name to "Google Drive OPP SL2"
4. Make a presentation using the sample provided on the next page.
    a. Be sure to enter your first and last name (capitalized) on the title slide.
    b. Enter your class name on your title slide.
    c. Slide numbers are not required. They are for instructional purposes only.
5. Rearrange order of slides 3-7 by moving at least one of these slides in the navigation pane. (It will no longer match the sample.)
. **Note**: Leave slides 1, 2 and 8 in their current order
6. Change the order of the bullets on slide 2 to match the slide titles in your new slide order
7. **Print** a 4-slide handout (or submit to your teacher per instructions for grading purposes).
    a. Staple the two pages together

Slide 1

Google Drive

by (Student Name)
(Class)

Slide 2

Google Drive

- Docs
- Sheets
- Slides
- Drawings
- Google Forms

Slide 3

Google Docs

- The online word processing program
- Saves instantly to your Google Drive (online and/or on your computer)
- Share and collaborate
- Export as common Microsoft Office formats or PDF

Slide 4

Google Sheets

- Online Spreadsheet program
- Saves instantly to Google Drive
- Its strength is working with NUMBERS
- Share and collaborate

Slide 5

Google Slides

- Online presentation tool for making slides
- Add images, charts and video
- Shares instantly to Google Drive
- Share and collaborate

Slide 6

Google Drawings

- Online drawing program
- Create drawings separately or use in other Documents

Slide 7

Google Forms

- Makes an online form which puts resulting data into a Google Sheet
- Easy to create and share
- Multiple choice
- Range questions (i.e. rank 1 to 5)
- Short answer
- Multiple answer (check boxes)
- Saves to Google Drive

Slide 8

Sharing Options

- View only or Edit permissions
- Private only
- Access with a link
- Access by invitation
- Public
- Login can be required or not

Lesson SL3: Images, WordArt, Change Background

"A picture is worth a thousand words." ~ Early 20th Century Adage

In addition to text, you can also add **images** and **WordArt** to your slides. Graphics like these can be very effective in communicating your message to your audience. More complex concepts can be better illustrated with a well-chosen image than it can be explained with words. Some of the most effective slides are nothing but an image.

Images:

Below is the **Insert Image** box. Let's see how it works. To bring up this box, go to the **Insert** menu in Google Docs and choose **Image**. The box will look like the following.

The options on the left are to indicate the source of your image. You can **Upload** an image from your computer or **Take a snapshot** using your computer's camera. You can also get images **By URL** (Uniform Resource Locator) if you enter (or copy/paste) the direct web address to an image that lives on the Internet. If you use Google's Picasa Albums you can select **Your albums** and navigate to the desired image. If you choose Google Drive, you can find an image from your Google Drive storage area. **Search**, the last option, allows you to search the Internet for images which have no copyright restrictions concerning its use.

The search option also gives you additional options for searching for images by **Any Type, Faces, Photo, Clip Art** and **Line Drawing**. **Clip Art** have limited colors and can be sized up better than other images found on the Internet. After your initial search, you can narrow down your search using the type options and colors found in the image using the color boxes at the top of the box. Once you have found an image you like, click the image then click the **Select** button at the bottom of the Insert Image box. The image will now be inserted as a floating graphic on your slide.

Once you have placed your image, you can use the sizing handles (in the corner of the selected image) to change its size. You can also move the graphic by dragging it by the border of the selection box. Above the selection box is a single rotation handle. Simply drag it left or right to rotate the image as desired.

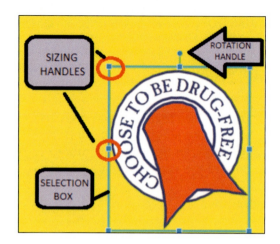

WordArt

WordArt is a way to create a graphic object which is based upon text. To create a WordArt, go to the Insert menu and select WordArt. In the box that appears (see figure at left), type the desired text and press **ENTER** to place it as a graphic on your slide. Once created, the graphic can be colorized and manipulated in the same ways as any graphic. WordArt is great for communicating excitement about your topic.

Background:

Each slide can have a color, pattern or image as a background. You can see your options in the dialog box to the right. You can change the background color or choose an image using the familiar **Insert Image** box discussed at the beginning of this lesson. You can also reset all backgrounds to the default for the chosen theme. If you click the "**Apply to all**" button, your change will affect all your slides. If you simply click the "**Done**" button, you only change the current slide.

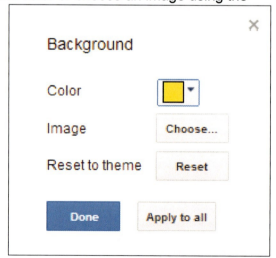

Tip: Make sure you choose a background color or image which does not compete visually with your slide content. If it does, you can choose a different background or change the colors of the text and other content on your slide so that you can read it easily. Allow enough contrast between your light and dark colored content.

Google Drive Essentials, George Somers

Let's make our slides more visually appealing in this tutorial.

1. Log in to Google Drive, **Make a copy** of Red Ribbon Week (File > Make a Copy) and save with the name "**Red Ribbon Lesson 3**".
2. Let's put some **WordArt** on our title slide.
   a. Go to Insert > WordArt.
   b. Enter "Say No to Drugs" in the WordArt dialog box that appears.
   c. Press the **ENTER** key (or **RETURN** on Mac's).
   d. With the WordArt selected on your slide, change the font, color and style using the buttons on the toolbar (see figure below). You can also experiment with line colors and line thicknesses and other settings as well.

   e. Drag the selection box of the WordArt to move the WordArt to the right corner.
   f. Choose corner sizing handle and make the WordArt small enough to work well in the upper right corner.
   g. Use the **rotation handle** on the WordArt to rotate it right about 22 degrees.
3. Now, let's put an image on Slide 2.
   a. Click Slide 2 in the navigation pane on the left side of your screen.
   b. Go to the **Insert** menu and select **Image.**
   c. In the **Insert Image dialog box**, do a **Search** for "red ribbon" (Tip: select RED for color).
   d. Click on an image that works well for our topic and click the **SELECT** button.
   e. Resize the image to make it smaller and drag it to the bottom right corner.
4. Let's try changing the background.
   a. Click on Slide 2 in the navigation pane on the left side of our screen.
   b. Click the **Background** button on the toolbar.
   c. Click the "Choose" button and search for "pattern". Use RED color search to narrow your search.
   d. Find a pattern you like and click the **Select** button.
   e. Apply the new background to your current slide or all the slides as desired.

4. Play your slide show on the computer by clicking on Slide 1 and clicking the "Present" button at the top of your window. Press **ESCAPE** key (ESC) to exit slide show.
5. Using the process in Step 3, add another image to Slide 6 similar to the sample below. Size and position the image as shown below.

Lesson SL3 Sample

   Note: Slides 3 and 4 are not shown.

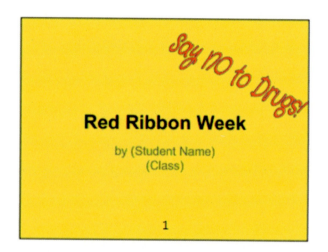

Wonderful work! You are now ready for **Opportunity SL3**. Venture on!

Opportunity SL3

1. Log in to your Google Drive account and create a new presentation.
2. Use the **Simple Light** theme to get started.
3. Click the document name ("Untitled Presentation") and change the name to "OPP SL3".
4. On your title slide enter "About Me" for the title placeholder.
5. For the subtitle, enter your first and last name on the first line and the name of your class. (See sample provided)
6. Create a new slide using the **BLANK** layout. (Hint: use the down-arrow of the new slide button and choose "Blank".)
7. Insert a **WordArt** using a word that describes you.
8. Repeat step 7 to insert two more **WordArt's** using words that describe you.
9. Scale and rotate your **WordArt's** to match the sample provided.
10. Insert another slide with the **Title Only** layout and enter "Places I Want to Visit" as your slide title.
11. On this slide, insert 2 or 3 images of places you would like to visit. Size them to look good on the slide. *If you cannot find the images you want using Image Search in Google Drive, search on google.com/images and copy the URL (link) to the FULL SIZE image. Paste the link into the "By URL" box in Insert Images. Ask your teacher for help with this.*
12. Insert labels for each image using **WordArt** to identify each place. For each one, use a different font and color.
13. Insert another slide with the **Title Only** layout and enter "People I'd Like to Meet" as your slide title.
14. On this slide, insert 2 or 3 images of people you would like to meet (alive or dead). Size them to look good on the slide. *If you cannot find the images you want using Image Search in Google Drive, search on google.com/images and copy the URL (link) to the FULL SIZE image. Paste the link into the "By URL" box in Insert Images. Ask your teacher for help with this.*
15. As before, add labels for each image using WordArt to identify each person. For each one, use a different font and color.

16. Choose one or more of your slides and change the background to a different color or image. Please choose a background that contrasts well with the text and other content on the slide.
17. Submit to your teacher for grading purposes per instructions.

Lesson SL4: Transitions, Animations, and Viewing Slideshows

When something we are viewing moves, it is called an animation. Google Slides has two ways to add animations to your presentations. Things that move on a slide are called **Animations**, while the movement you see BETWEEN slides is call an **Animation**. We will discuss both of the ways to make things move on the screen in this lesson. When used properly and in moderation, animations can be very effective in communicating your message to your audience.

Slide Transitions:

Google Slides offers several ways to exit one slide and bring in the next. You can choose from a list of animations, control the speed using a slider and get a preview of what the animation might look like when in presentation mode. Feel free to experiment with the setting to find a transition that works well with your presentation. Simply select the slide to which you want to add a transition and click the Transitions button on the toolbar to get started.

Transition Choices **Transition Options**

Google Drive Essentials, George Somers

Animations:

You can also make objects on your slide move. You can even have multiple objects move on your slide all at once or individually in a desired sequence. As with transitions, you can set you preferences in the Animations pane (see the figure above on the right). We'll explore these options in this lesson.

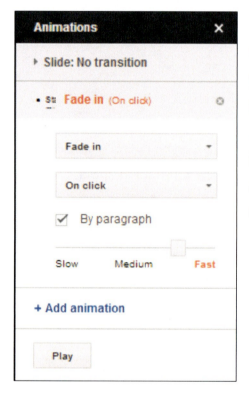

You can animate a graphic, WordArt, text block or individual lines (or paragraphs) within the text block. Once the animations pane is open, you can select the object to be animated and choose your animation options. In addition to speed, you can also customize the trigger for the animation, decide to animate "by paragraph" and add additional transitions to the same or other objects on your slide.

Playing your Presentation:

To view your slides, animations and transitions in their full glory, you should **Present** your slideshow full screen. You should note that clicking the **Present** button will show your slides from the current slide. To play your slides from the beginning, click the down-arrow on the **Present**

button and choose **Present from beginning**. Once in presentation mode, you can advance your slides by clicking the mouse button, pressing the right arrow key on the keyboard, or pressing the spacebar. You can move to the previous slide by pressing the left arrow key on the keyboard.

Let's learn how animations and transitions work in a presentation.

1. Log in to Google Drive and open your original Red Ribbon Week presentation.
2. **Make a copy** of Red Ribbon Week (File > Make Copy) and save with the name "Red Ribbon Lesson 4".
3. In the Navigation pane (on the left), select slide 2.
4. Click the "**Animations**" button on the toolbar.
5. Select a slide animation of your choice from the drop-down menu and choose the desired speed.
6. Click the **PLAY** button in the Animations pane to see a preview.
7. Press the **STOP** button when the animation is complete.
8. Note: Do not close the Animation pane at this time. If you do close it, you can reopen it again by pressing the **Animations** button.
9. In the Navigation Pane (left), select slide 3.
10. Click on the first line of bullet points to put the insertion point at the first bullet point of text.
11. In the ANIMATIONS pane (right side), click on "Add Animation".
12. Choose desired text animation and speed.
13. Check the "By Paragraph" box to have each line enter or exit on a mouse click.
14. Preview the animation by clicking the "PLAY" button in the Animations Pane. You can see each animation on the slide by clicking the mouse on the slide area of the screen. Press the "STOP" button when all animations have completed.
15. Now, select Slide 6 in the Navigation Pane (left).
16. Insert an image like the one below and select it.

17. In the Animations pane, add animation to the image. Use "with previous setting" as the trigger (see figure at right).
18. For remaining slides, add slide, text, and image animations. Feel free to experiment with animation options, including speed.
19. **Note**: If you wish to remove an animation, simply click the **X** next to the name of the animation in the Animations pane (on right).
20. Show your completed presentation by clicking the "Present" button (use drop-down menu to choose Start from beginning). Use your space bar or mouse to advance to each new animation.

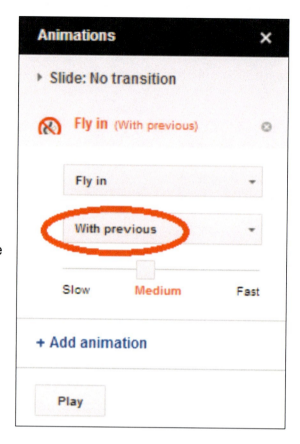

Good job! You are now ready for **Opportunity SL4.**

Opportunity SL4

1. Log in to your Google Drive account and open your "OPP SL3" file.
2. **MAKE A COPY** of it and **NAME** it "OPP SL4".
3. Go to Slide 2, click the Transitions button to open the Transitions Pane and add an animation for each of the words about yourself.
4. Go to Slide 4 and add a new slide using the "Title and Body" layout.
5. In the Title placeholder, type "My Favorite Movies". It is not necessary to include a slide number at the bottom of the slide. (See sample below)
6. In the Content placeholder, make a bulleted list of 4 or 5 of your favorite movies. [*Hint: Be sure to capitalize in title case. Example: Pirates of the Caribbean.*]
7. For each line in your bulleted list, add an animation so that each line enters and/or exits the slide individually activated by a mouse click. [*Hint: use "by paragraph" option.*]
8. Finally, add a slide transition to any 3 of your slides.
9. Show your completed slideshow to your teacher or submit as directed for grading purposes.

Favorite Movies

- Wall-E
- Monsters, Inc.
- WarGames
- Pixar Shorts
- Harry Potter

Lesson SL5: Tables

Tables are a great way to display data in a document or a slide. Google Slides makes it easy to create tables for your presentation. Tables are defined as a grid of cells. When you create a Table, you indicate how many rows and columns you need in your table. Plus, you can add or remove columns and rows as needed from the **Table menu** as needed after you have created it (see figure at right).

You can also make your table more visually appealing by adding cell[13] color fill, borders and border colors using the buttons found on the toolbar (see figure below).

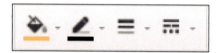

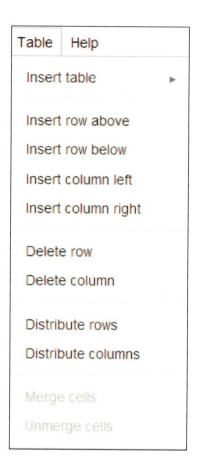

In this lesson, you will learn how to create and format tables in Google Slides.

Let's get started!

1. Login to Google Drive and create a new presentation.
2. Select a theme of your choice. The sample at the end of this lesson uses the "Simple Light" theme.
3. Click on the name of the presentation (upper right corner) and name it "Lesson SL5".
4. On the title slide, enter "Computers" as the title and "Input and Output" for the subtitle.
5. Create a **new slide** using the "Blank" layout. Be sure to click on the down-arrow on the new slide button to choose your layout.

---

[13] As described in the Google Sheets section of this book, cells are the boxes formed at the intersection of a row and a column.

6. Go to the Table menu and create a 2x4 table by going to Insert Table and using your mouse to select the size of your table.

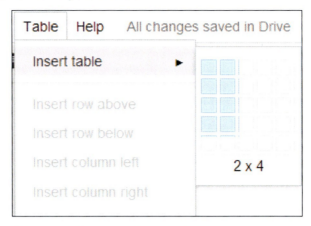

7. Type the text "Input" in your first row, first column.
8. Type the word "Output" in the first row, second column.
9. Practice using the arrow keys on your keyboard to move from cell to cell.
10. Finish the first column with the text "Keyboard", "Mouse" and "Touchscreen Monitor" in each cell respectively (see sample at the end of this lesson).
11. Finish the second column with the text "Monitor (Regular)", "Printer" and "Speakers" in each cell respectively (see sample).
12. Now, let's make and outside border for the top row:
    a. Select the top two cells by dragging your mouse through the cells.
    b. From the drop-down arrow in the "Output" box, choose **Select outer border**. A blue box will appear around both cells indicating that the borders are selected.
    c. Change the cell borders to 3px (3 pixels) using **line thickness button**.
    d. With the border still selected, change the color to a color of your choice using the **line color button** on the toolbar.
    e. Click outside the table to deselect it and see how it looks so far.
13. Once again, highlight your top row by dragging through the text.
14. Change your fill color to any color you wish using the **fill color button**. Make sure you can still read the text.

15. Let's add 1 more row to our table. Here's how:
    a. Click in one of the cells in the last row.
    b. Go to the **Table** menu and select **Insert Row Below**. A new row will be created.
    c. Enter the text "Scanner" as another input device.
16. Now, we need to change Font Sizes
    a. Select table by doing the following:
        i. Click anywhere in the first cell with the text "Input".
        ii. Then, click on the outside border of the table to select it.
    b. Change your font size to 24. You can also change the fonts and font colors as desired.
17. Let's try resizing the table:
    a. Drag the left table border to the right about 1 inch (see sample).
    b. Drag the right table border to the left about 1 inch (see sample).
    c. Drag the bottom border down about so it covers about ⅔ of the slide (see sample).

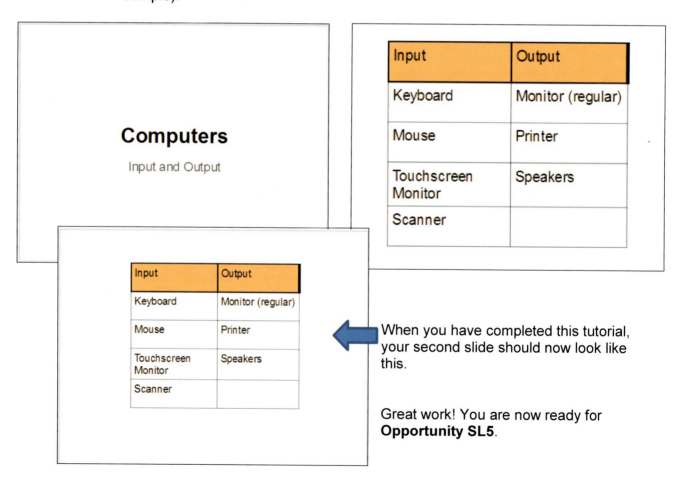

When you have completed this tutorial, your second slide should now look like this.

Great work! You are now ready for **Opportunity SL5**.

Opportunity SL5

1. Log in to your Google Drive account and open your "OPP SL4".
2. **MAKE A COPY** of it and **RENAME** it "OPP SL5".
3. Make a new slide 6 using the "Title only" layout.
4. For the title, enter the text "My Favorite Books"
5. Insert a two-column by four-row ("2 by 4") table.
6. At the top of the first column, enter the text "Title". *Be sure to use Title case.*
7. At the top of the second column, enter the text "Author". *Be sure to use Title case.*
8. Complete the table by entering the titles and authors of your at least 3 of your favorite books. Use the Internet as needed. Add additional rows as needed.
9. Add one additional book called "The Book of My Life". Enter your name for the author.
10. Add a third column. In the first column, first row enter the text "Rating (1-10)"
11. In the third column of the table, enter a rating for each book in your list.
12. Make the left column of your table wider than the other two columns.
13. Add 2 different border colors and thicknesses in your table.
14. Include at least 2 different fill colors and text colors in your table.
15. Make your table bigger by resizing the left, right and bottom borders of your table. Make the table slightly smaller than the slide area below the title.
16. Increase your font size by at least two sizes.
17. Compare your last slide to the sample on the next page.
18. Submit to your teacher per instructions.

My Favorite Books

Title	Author	Rating
The Hobbit	JRR Tolkien	9
The Last Lecture	Randy Pausch	9
Windows 7 Secrets	Paul Thurrott	8
The Book of My Life	George Somers	10

Lesson SL6: Speaker Notes

Speaker Notes allow you to make some notes for yourself, the speaker, about each slide. With Speaker Notes, you can add additional information that you can't or don't wish to put on your slide or simply give yourself some helpful reminders.

At the bottom of each Google Slides screen, you will find the Notes Area (see below). In this section of your window, you can enter your notes for each slide. Later, you can print these notes along with the corresponding slide to use during your presentation.

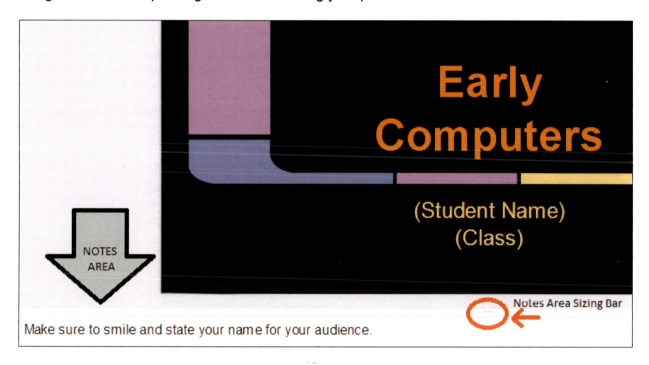

In this tutorial, we'll create a simple, 7-slide presentation. Most of these slides will have only a title and an image. You, the speaker, will be able to use your notes to give details about the images you show. Let's see how speaker notes work.

1. Login to Google Drive and create a **new** presentation.
2. Select "Trek" as your **theme** and **rename** it "Lesson SL6".
3. On the title slide enter the text "Early Computers" in your title placeholder and enter your name and class name in the subtitle placeholder (see sample at the end of this tutorial).
4. Using the sizing bar (see figure above), resize the **Notes Area** of the screen so that it is approximately 4 lines of text high.
5. Enter the text "Make sure to smile and state your name for your audience." in the **Notes Area** of your first slide.

6. Complete the remaining slides according to the sample using the following steps:
    a. Create a new slide using the "Title Only" layout.
    b. Enter the name and year for each computer.
    c. Using **Insert>Image**, search for the image shown using the name of the computer and the year as search terms.
    d. Select the desired image to place it in your slide.
    e. Resize and move the image on the slide so that it matches the sample.
    f. Enter the text for the Notes Area as shown on the sample.
7. In Google Drive's File menu, select "Print Settings and Preview".
8. In the toolbar, set the preview to "1 slide with notes" as shown below.

9. Print your slide notes if your teacher requests that you do so.

Sample: Slide 1

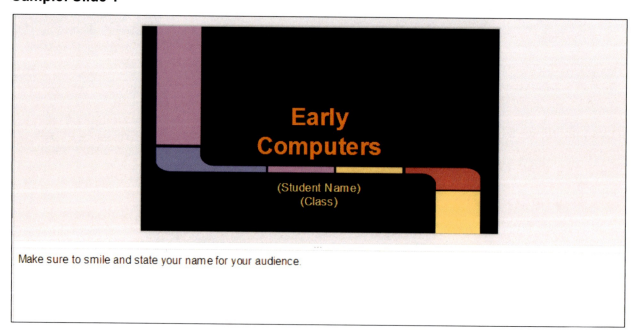

Sample: Slide 2

Charles Babbage proposed the first general mechanical computer known as the Analytical Engine in 1837. It had an Arithmetic Logic Unit (ALU), basic flow control, and integrated memory and is the first general-purpose computer concept. Unfortunately, he couldn't afford to build the machine. However, his son In 1910, Henry Babbage, Charles Babbage's youngest son, was able to complete a portion of this machine and was able to make it do basic calculations successfully.

Sample: Slide 3

The ENIAC was invented by J. Presper Eckert and John Mauchly at the University of Pennsylvania. It took 3 years to build and was completed in 1946. It occupied about 1,800 square feet. It had 18,000 vacuum tubes and weighed nearly 50 tons. Many consider the ENIAC to be the first digital computer because it was fully functional.

Sample: Slide 4

Ed Roberts created the term "personal computer" when he launched the Altair 8800 in 1975. A series of switches were used for inputting data and output data. The switched would turn on and off a series of lights.

Sample: Slide 5

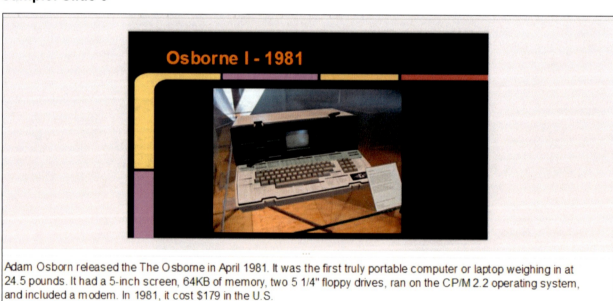

Adam Osborn released the The Osborne in April 1981. It was the first truly portable computer or laptop weighing in at 24.5 pounds. It had a 5-inch screen, 64KB of memory, two 5 1/4" floppy drives, ran on the CP/M 2.2 operating system, and included a modem. In 1981, it cost $179 in the U.S.

Sample: Slide 6

Steve Wozniak and Steve Jobs designed the first Apple known as the Apple I computer in 1976 which used a form of the BASIC operating system and used a television as a display. The widely popular Apple II was released in 1977. In 1984, Apple launched the Macintosh. The Mac used its own windowed operating system and a mouse pointing device.

Sample: Slide 7

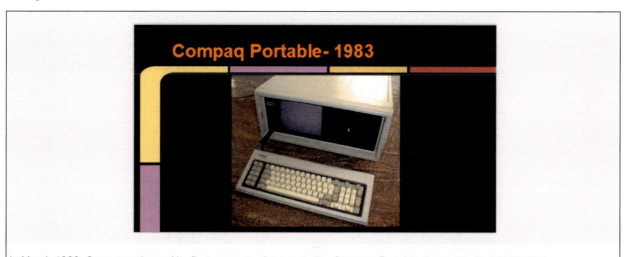

In March 1983, Compaq released its first computer known as the Compaq Portable. It was the first 100% IBM compatible computer. At the time, it cost $2995 with a single 5.25 inch floppy disk drive and $3590 with two disk drives. It was an early all-in-one computer.

Nice job! You are now ready for Opportunity SL6.

Opportunity SL6

1. Login to Google Drive and open your "**OPP SL4**" presentation.
2. Make a copy and name it "OPP SL6".
3. In the **Notes Area** for Slide 2, type 2 or 3 sentences about why you choose the words on that slide.
4. In the **Notes Area** for Slide 3, type 1 or 2 sentences for each location about why you want to visit the places you chose.
5. In the **Notes Area** for Slide 4, type 1 or 2 sentences for each person about why you would want to (or would have liked to) meet the people you put on that slide.
6. In the **Notes Area** for Slide 5, type 2 or 3 sentences about your favorite movie from your list. Explain why you like that movie so much.
7. In Google Drive's File menu, select "Print Settings and Preview".
8. In the toolbar, set the preview to "1 slide with notes".
9. Print your notes and/or submit as directed to your teacher for grading purposes.

Lesson SL7: Buttons and Hyperlinks

Creating a group of slides which show in order, one after the other, is what you need for many types of presentations. Some presentations, however, require the ability to jump to a slide other than the next slide. To do this you need a **hyperlink**.

Hyperlinks allow you to jump to another slide in your presentation by clicking some linked text or a button. Hyperlinks are the basis of how we navigate the World Wide Web. In Google Slides, a hyperlink can link to a slide in your presentation or another website using its address in the form of a URL (Uniform Resource Locator).

Hyperlinks can attached to a string of text or a graphic object, such as a shape (e.g. a button) or an image. When in **Present** mode, the mouse pointer becomes a pointing finger (see figure at right) to show you the object is clickable. In this lesson, you'll learn how to make hyperlinks out of these objects and learn how to link them to slides and websites.

Using the sample provided at the end of this tutorial, make a trivia quiz by doing the following steps.

1. Create a new presentation in Google Drive.
2. Choose the **Simple Light** theme.
3. For the name of the file, change "Untitled Presentation" to "Lesson SL7".
4. On the Title slide, enter "Trivia Quiz" for the title and *your name* and *your class name* for the subtitle.
5. Create a new slide using the **Title only** layout.
6. In the Title for slide 2 (your new slide), enter "In what year did Google become an incorporated company?"
7. Using the **Research** pane (Tools > Research), find the answer to this question. *(Hint: search on "History of Google")*
8. Insert a text box on your slide (Insert > text box). Draw a rectangle on your slide and add a fill/border color. Size the text box as desired (see sample).
9. Click on your "button" and use copy/paste to create 3 more text boxes. These will be your "buttons" for the answers.

10. In your text boxes, enter answer options. Make sure that one of the "buttons" is the correct answer.
11. Make a new blank slide for the correct answer reveal. Using WordArt, put a large "Correct" on your slide. Change font, color and other style options as desired.
12. We now need to link the button with the correct answer to Slide 3. Here's how:
    a. Go back to slide 2 and select the text box with the correct answer. (Hint: Click the border of the "button" to select the entire object, not just the text.)
    b. Choose Insert>Link from Google Drive's menu bar.
    c. In **Link To** box, click the triangle to the left of **Slide in this presentation**.

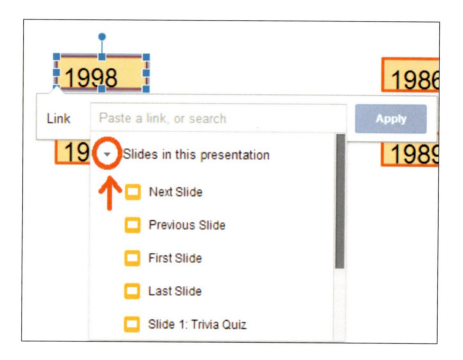

    d. In the Slide list, scroll down the list and select **Slide 3** from the list.
    e. Click the Apply button when you are done.
13. Now, let's make the slide for an incorrect answer:
    a. Make another blank slide (slide 4)
    a. Add WordArt (as before) with the word "Incorrect".
    b. Insert a text box (as before) with the words "Try Again".
    c. Add a link from this text box to Slide 2.
    d. Make all text boxes with the wrong answer link to Slide 4.

14. Let's test out your trivia quiz using all answer choices.
    a. Go to slide 1.
    b. Click the Present button to enter presentation mode.
    c. Test your link for the correct and incorrect answers from Slide 2.
15. You can make a hyperlink to a website too! Here's how:
    a. At the bottom of Slide 3, add a text box using the words "More info."
    b. Add coloring and borders as desired.
    c. Click the border of your "button" to select it.
    d. Now let's link this button to the website on which you found the answer to your question.
        1. Go back to the Research pane. If it is closed, open it again by going to **Tools > Research**.
        2. Right-click the link to the website and choose "Copy link address" from the menu that appears.
        3. Select Insert > Link from the Google Drive menu.
        4. Paste the website address into the Link box and click **Apply**.
16. Go to Slide 1 and **Present** your presentation again to test all of your links, including the new "More info" button we just added.

See the sample for this lesson on the next page.

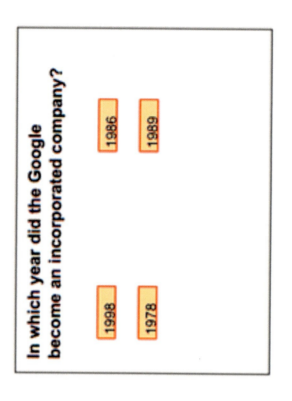
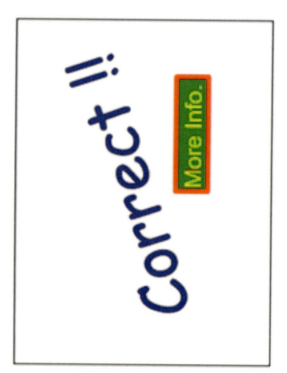

Great! You are now ready for Opportunity SL7.

Opportunity SL7
Buttons and Hyperlinks

Using the sample as a guide:

1. Create a new blank presentation in Google Drive.
2. Select the **Simple Light** theme and **Rename** your presentation "OPP SL7".
3. On your title slide, enter "Saving Energy and Money at Home" as the title and **your name** for the subtitle.
4. Add a new slide using the **blank** layout.
5. Go to **Insert > Image**. Use the **By URL** option and enter http://goo.gl/s70ng as the URL. You will see the outline of a house. *Note: this URL is case sensitive so capitalize as indicated.*[14]
6. Widen the image to match sample provided.
7. Create slide 3 using the **Title and Body** layout and enter text as it is on the sample, including bulleted text.
8. Repeat the previous step for slides 4 and 5.
9. On slide 3,
    a. Use the **Insert>Text Box** command to create a button with the text "Home" in 36 point font.
    b. Click on the text box border and use the **Insert>Link** command to make the text box link back to slide 2 (see sample).
    c. Align the text to be centered horizontally and vertically.
    d. Add a colored border and shading (fill) as desired but allow enough contrast between the text and the fill.
    e. Use copy/paste command to copy this button to slides 4 and 5.
10. On slide 2,
    a. Make your first button for this slide to match the sample and customize border and fill colors as desired. Use a font size of at least 30 points.
    b. Use copy/paste command again to copy 3 more of these buttons onto your slide.
    c. Change the text of the buttons to match the sample. Be sure to align the text horizontally and vertically in the text box.

---

[14] For entry purposes, this is a shortened URL using the goo.gl service. It will point to the full address.

d. For all buttons except the "More Information" button, use the **Insert>Link** command to make each button link to the slide with the matching title.

   e. In similar fashion, make the "More Information" button link to http://goo.gl/EAzjy. *Note: this URL is case sensitive so capitalize as indicated.*

11. Finally, add a text box to the title slide with the text "Let's Get Started!", format it as desired and make it link to slide 2.
12. Test your presentation to make sure all links work.
13. Show your presentation and/or submit it to your teacher for grading purposes as per grading instructions.

Opportunity SL7 Sample:

Slide 1:

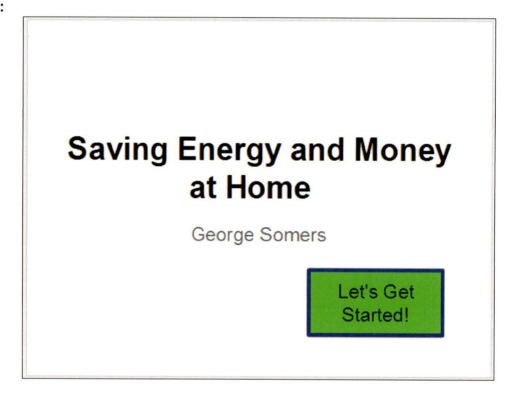

Slide 2:

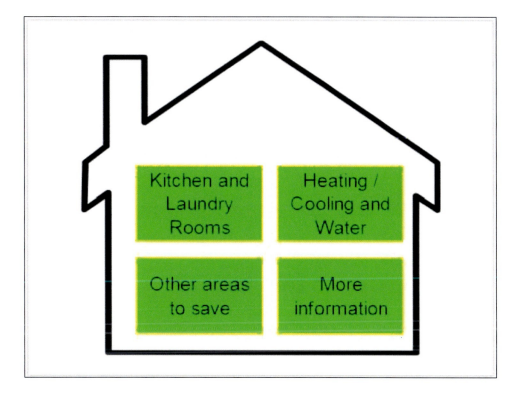

Slide 3:

Kitchen and Laundry Room

- Upgrade your refrigerator to a more energy efficient model (save 4%)
- Upgrade appliances to more energy efficient models (save 12+%)
- Air dry your dishes (save 3%)
- Wash clothes in cold, then let them air dry (9%)

Slide 4:

Heating/Cooling and Water

- Install ceiling fans (save 19%)
- Get a blanket for your water heater (save 1-3%)
- Plug air leaks in windows to keep warm air (in winter) and cool air (in summer) from escaping (save 12%)
- Use a programmable thermostat (save 10%)

HOME

Slide 5:

Other Areas to Save

- Turn off lights in rooms not being used (save 2%)
- Eliminate "phantom load" by turning off electronic gadgets and devices when not in use (save 5%)

HOME

GRAPHICS

GOOGLE DRAWINGS

Lesson GR1: Basic Shapes, Lines and Line Styles

Google Drive also has a basic drawing app called **Google Drawings**. You can create, edit and print drawings using universal tools found in many drawing and painting applications. You can place these drawings in a Google Docs document or export them for use in desktop applications. In this lesson, we'll learn about creating drawings using a combination of basic shapes, lines and line styles. Once these objects are drawn, they can be sized, edited and moved just like the images we have used in many lessons so far.

Google Drawings offers a variety of basic shapes. These shapes are drawn by dragging a mouse pointer which will look like ╋ to define the size and dimensions of your object. Simply drag your mouse pointer down and to the right to define an imaginary square on your screen. Your shape will appear matching the height and width of the square you defined. We can also add text to the shapes.

Here are the choices for **basic shapes** available from the toolbar:

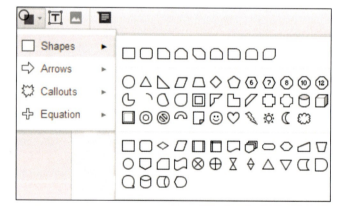

There are also line tools available. Since a line is defined as the shortest distance between two points, we can make a straight line by starting our mouse drag from the point at which we want the line to start and ending where we want it to end. The figure at the right shows the available **line** choices. You can even create **scribbles** by dragging the mouse to define the point of your line.

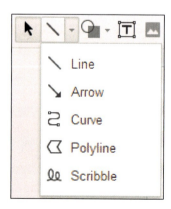

Once you have created a line, you can adjust the line color (#1 in figure below), weight or thickness (#2), line dash style (#3), arrowhead start (#4) and arrowhead end type (#5) for your line. These options are available by clicking on your line object and using the tools found in the toolbar to adjust its settings.

Let's see these basic shape and line tools in action with the following tutorial.

Using the instructions below, create a drawing similar to the sample shown at the end of this tutorial.

1. Login in to Google Drive and create a new **Google Drawings** document using the **New > More** submenu.
2. Rename your drawing file "Lesson GR1".
3. Go to the basic shapes menu on the tool bar and select the **rectangle shape**.
4. In the upper left corner of your drawing area, draw a rectangle by dragging your mouse pointer down and to the right to define the height and width of your rectangle.

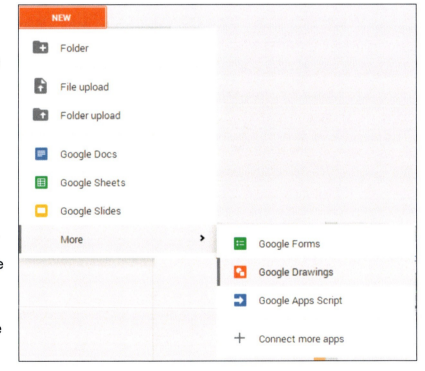

5. We can use this same tool to draw a square. Since a square is simply a rectangle with the same height and width we can use the rectangle tool to draw a perfect square. Here's how:
    a. Select the rectangle tool from the tool bar.

b. Go to the bottom left corner of your drawing area, hold down the SHIFT key on your keyboard and draw out your square. Using the SHIFT key lock the height and width to make a perfect square.

6. In the center of your drawing area, draw an oval using the oval tool under the shapes tools.
7. We have decided it would be better to have a perfect circle so let's remove the oval and draw a circle instead. Here's how:
a. Click on the oval you just drew and press the DELETE/BACKSPACE key on your keyboard to delete the oval.
b. Now, select the oval shape tool again but draw your circle while holding down the SHIFT key on your keyboard.
8. There is actually a **Smiley Face** tool available in our shapes so there is no need to draw the eyes and mouth on our face. Use the same method as in the step above, delete the circle you just drew and draw a Smiley Face in its place while holding down the SHIFT key on your keyboard to make it a perfect circle.
9. You will see a yellow diamond in the middle of the Smiley Face's mouth. This is an edit point which you can drag up and down to change the shape of the mouth. Drag it up a bit until the mouth is a flat line.
10. Let's use the line tool to give our face a simple mustache. Here's how:
    a. Select a straight line from the **Select Line** button on the toolbar.
    b. Draw a line by dragging from left to right in your drawing area where you want the mustache to be. You will now have a line with two sizing handles at the endpoints. These can be used to change the direction and length of your line.
    c. When the line is selected you will see the new line options appear on the toolbar like this:
    d. Click the **Line Color** button and change the color of your line to red (or a color of your choice).
    e. Click the **Line Weight** button and change the line thickness to **8px**. This will set the thickness to 8 pixels. The bigger number of pixels, the thicker your line will be.
    f. Click the Arrowhead Start button and change the beginning of the line to a filled circle.
    g. Click the Arrowhead End button and change the end of the line to filled circle.
    h. Click somewhere else in your drawing to deselect the line and see how it looks. Feel free to experiment with the settings until you like how your line looks.

11. Now, let's make a thought bubble.
    a. From the **Shapes** button on the toolbar, get a **Cloud Callout** from the **Callouts** category of shapes.
    b. Draw a Cloud Callout in the upper right corner of your drawing area the same way you would draw out a circle or a square.
    c. Right-click the cloud you just drew and select "**Edit Text**" from the menu that appears.
    d. Type the text "I'm hungry" in the cloud.
    e. Highlight the text and adjust the font, size and color like you would with any text until you are satisfied with the thought bubble.
    f. Click somewhere else in your drawing area to deselect the object and see how it looks.
12. Make the starburst by following these steps.
    a. From the Shapes button on the toolbar, select the **Explosion 1** shape from the **Callouts** category of shapes.
    b. Draw out the explosion shape on the left size of your drawing area the same way you drew the cloud.
    c. Right-click the explosion object you just drew and select "**Edit Text**" from the menu that appears.
    d. Type the word "Bazinga!" and change the font, size and style to one of your choosing.
    e. Change the fill color of the object using the **Fill Color** button on the toolbar to select the color you want. Make sure you can still read it against your font color.
    f. Now click the border of your explosion shape to select the object again and change the line color.
    g. Change the line weight to a thicker setting.
    h. Set the line style to dash-dot (see figure at right)
    i. Experiment with your color and line objection until you are happy with them.

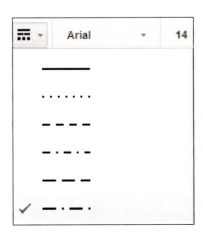

13. Finally, let's add our scribble at the top of our drawing. Here's how:
    a. From the **Select Line** button on the toolbar, select the Scribble tool.
    b. Draw out a scribbled line similar to the one in the sample at the top of your drawing area.
    c. Click somewhere else in your drawing to deselect the scribble object and see what the drawing now looks like.

Fun, huh? Nice job! Now try the Opportunity GR1 on the next page to see how you have mastered these new skills.

Opportunity GR1

Basic Shapes and Lines

1. Create a new Graphics document named **"OPP GR1"**.
2. Using the sample as a guide, create a graphic similar to the one below demonstrating the use of the following objects:
    a. rectangle
    b. square
    c. oval
    d. circle
    e. line
    f. arrow
    g. text on a shape
    h. scribble
3. Change the fill color of at least two of the objects.
4. Change the line color of at least two of the objects.
5. Change the line style of at least two of the objects.
6. Match the line thickness of the objects in the sample.
7. Center your text and increase the text size.
8. Add additional shapes as desired.
9. Print and/or share with your teacher as instructed for grading purposes.

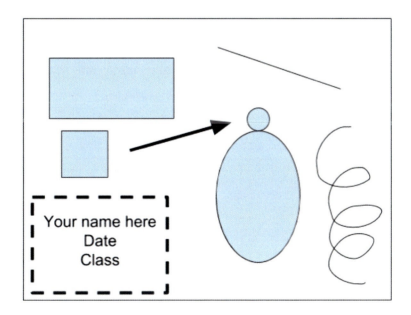

Lesson GR2: Draw, Duplicate, Rotate and Manipulate Complex Graphic Objects

In this lesson, we will learn more about working with more complex graphics objects. These graphics can be easily **duplicated** (or copied) and **rotated**. By duplicating an object, you can ensure that your copies are identical to the original. Shapes can then be combined for interesting effects. You can even change the attributes of some shapes using a yellow diamond **manipulation handle** (see right). In the second part of this lesson, we'll learn how to make more complicated objects using the **polygon tool**.

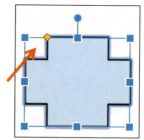

Let's give it a try. Using the sample at the end of this tutorial as a guide, complete the following tutorial.

1. Login in to Google Drive and create a new drawing document.
2. Rename the document "Lesson GR2 Part 1".
3. In the upper left corner of your drawing area, draw a perfect square. (Hint: hold down the SHIFT key while drawing a rectangle shape.)
4. To the right of that, draw a **Parallelogram** . See your shape choices in the figure at the right.
5. To the right of the Parallelogram, draw a **Trapezoid** 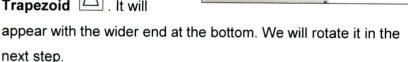. It will appear with the wider end at the bottom. We will rotate it in the next step.

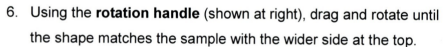
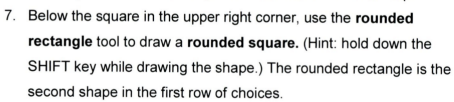

6. Using the **rotation handle** (shown at right), drag and rotate until the shape matches the sample with the wider side at the top.
7. Below the square in the upper right corner, use the **rounded rectangle** tool to draw a **rounded square**. (Hint: hold down the SHIFT key while drawing the shape.) The rounded rectangle is the second shape in the first row of choices.

8. To the right of the rounded square, draw a **Hexagon** (six-sided polygon) .
9. To the right of the Hexagon, draw a **Triangle** .

10. Below the rounded square, draw a **Right Triangle** .
11. Now, let's duplicate and rotate the Hexagon.
    a. Click on the Hexagon to select it.
    b. From Google Drive's **Edit** menu, select **Duplicate** to make a copy of the Hexagon.
    c. Drag the copy below the original Hexagon and rotate it to make the sample below.

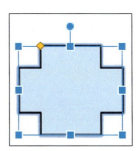

12. Below the triangle, draw a cross. Drag the yellow triangle handle (see figure at right) to manipulate the cross until it matches the sample at the end of the tutorial.
13. To the right of the cross, draw a **Pentagon**.
14. Lastly, draw a Cube in the upper right corner of your drawing area and manipulate it using the yellow diamond handle until it matches the sample.
15. Close your "Lesson GR2 Part 1" document and proceed with the next part of this lesson below.

Polygons are irregular shapes. They can have any number of sides and tend to be non-symmetrical in nature. Instead of drawing an imaginary rectangle on the screen to define a polygon's height and width, as you do with rectangles and circles, you define the shape by clicking the mouse to mark each of its corners. When you are done with each corner, click back on the first corner you created and it will become a completed, closed shape. You can then manipulate it as you can any other shape.

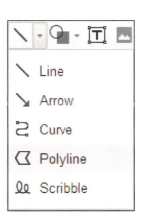

16. In Google Drive, create a new drawing document and **rename** it "Lesson GR2 Part 2".
17. From the Line menu, select the polyline tool (see figure at right)
18. Draw a polygon using the sample on the next page as a guide. Here's how:
    a. Click somewhere in your drawing area to define the first corner.
    b. Move the mouse somewhere else in the drawing area and click to define a second corner.
    c. Repeat step 18b until all the corners of your object are created.
    d. Click on the first corner you created to complete and close the shape.

Google Drive Essentials, George Somers

19. **Duplicate** the shape (Hint: Edit > Duplicate).
20. Modify the colors and line of the duplicate polygon as desired.
21. Move the new polygon over the original as shows in the sample. This will create a shadow effect.
22. Close this drawing document.

Lesson GR2 Part 1

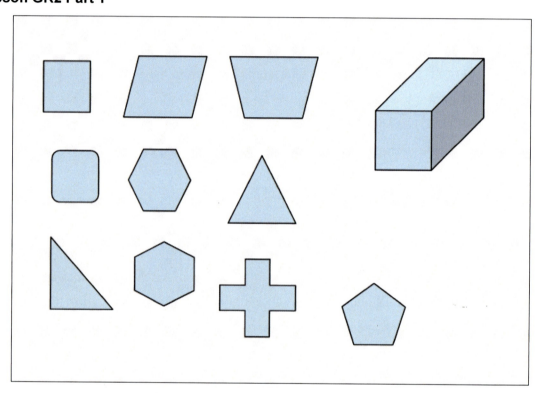

Lesson GR2 Part 2

Good work! You are now ready for Opportunity GR2 on the next page.

Opportunity GR2

Draw, duplicate, and manipulate more complex objects.

1. Create a new **Google Docs document**[15] named **"OPP GR2"** or as instructed by your teacher.
2. Type your assignment header as directed by your teacher.
3. Press ENTER (RETURN) key two times.
4. Select **Drawing** from the **Insert** menu and draw the following, then click **Save and Close** button.

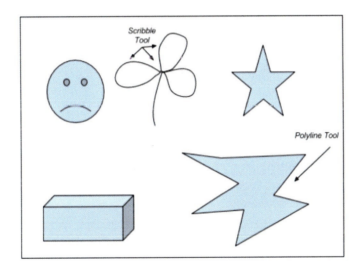

5. Press ENTER (RETURN) key two times.

(continued on next page)

---

[15] Note: not a Drawing file type

6. Select **Drawing** from the **Insert** menu and draw the following. Do not close your drawing until step 7.

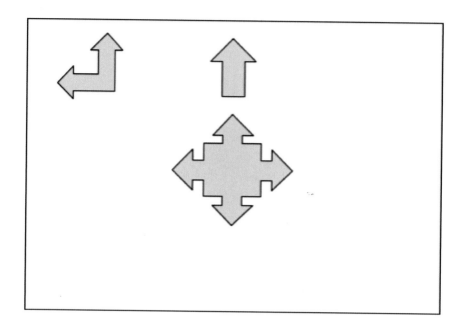

7. Duplicate the original arrow and bent arrow as needed to make your drawing look like the following, then click **Save and Close** button.

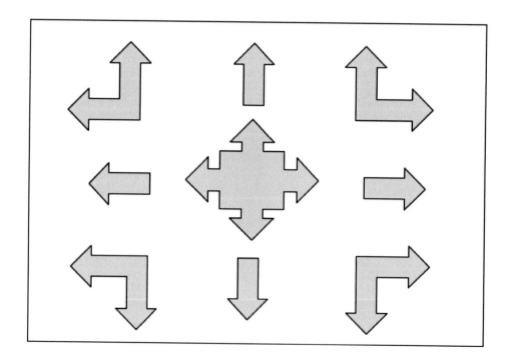

8. Submit as required by your teacher.

Lesson GR3: Alignment

Sometimes, when combining multiple shapes into a drawing, you will need to arrange objects so that they line up vertically (i.e. up and down) and/or horizontally (i.e. left to right). This is known as vertical and horizontal alignment. See the figures below for examples of both alignments.

Vertical Alignment

Horizontal Alignment

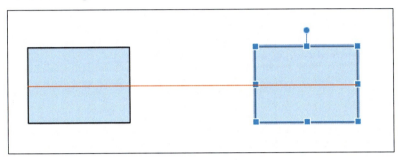

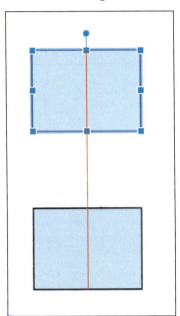

Google Drawings gives you two ways to align objects. The first is by revealing a red **guiding line** to use as you drag the second object into place. You can see these guiding lines in the examples shown here.

The second way that Google Drawings helps you to align objects is by using the Arrange menu. Once you have selected two or more objects to align, select the desired alignment option from the Arrange menu as shown below.

Options for Aligning Objects Vertically

Options for Aligning Objects Horizontally

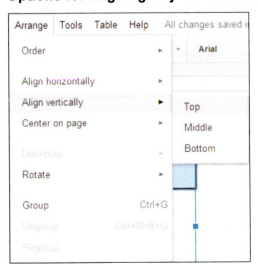

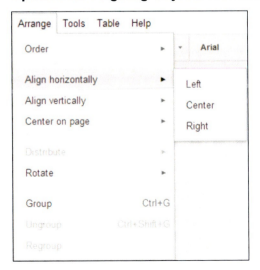

Google Drive Essentials, George Somers

Now let's see these commands in action with the tutorial below.

1. **Create** a new drawing document and **rename** it "Lesson GR3".
2. In your drawing space, draw a **rectangle**.
3. **Duplicate** the rectangle using Edit > Duplicate.
4. Drag the duplicate rectangle to the right of the first one and use the red guiding line to align them vertically.
5. **Duplicate** the <u>original</u> rectangle using Edit > Duplicate.
6. Draw the new rectangle below the first one and use the red guiding line to align it horizontally with the original. Your drawing should now look like the following:

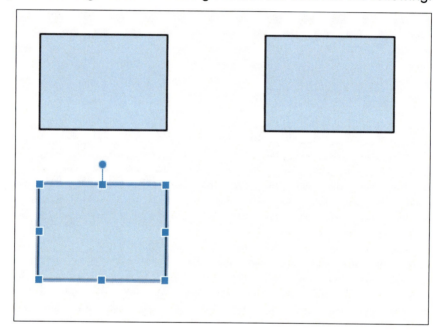

7. Delete the top row of rectangles. Here's how:
   a. Select the rectangle in the upper left corner by clicking it with the mouse.
   b. SHIFT-Click (i.e. Click while holding down a SHIFT key on the keyboard) the rectangle in the upper right corner. BOTH rectangles should now be selected.
   c. Press the BACKSPACE/DELETE key on the keyboard to delete both rectangles.
8. In the upper left corner of your drawing area, draw a **triangle**.
9. To the right of the triangle, draw an **oval**.
10. Drag the oval on top of the rectangle and use the red guiding line to align it to the center (vertically and horizontally) of the rectangle. It should now look something like the figure on the right.

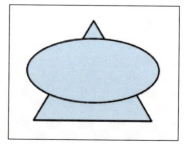

11. From Google Drive's **Edit** menu, choose **Select All** to select all objects in the drawing area.
12. From the **Arrange** menu, choose **Align vertically > Bottom** to align the objects vertically. The bottom of all the objects will be the align point.

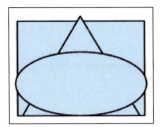

13. From the **Arrange** menu, choose **Align horizontally > Center**. The objects will now be centered with one another horizontally. Your drawing will now look like the figure at the right.

Nice job! Proceed with the Opportunity GR3 on the next page.

Opportunity GR3

Do you want to build a snowman?

1. Create a new drawing and **rename** it "OPP GR3".
2. Using the sample below, create a snowman. Keep the following requirements in mind as you create your drawing:
    a. The three body sections should be ovals and should be aligned horizontally centered with one another.
    b. Add a hat and buttons using shaped drawing tools of your choice. These should also be aligned centered with the snowman's body.
    c. Add a mouth to the face using a shape or drawing tool of our choice. Align it horizontally centered with the snowman's body. (Hint: the sample uses a crescent moon which is rotated to 270 degrees.)
    d. Add an ornament to the hat using a shape of your choice and align it horizontally centered with the snowman's body.
    e. Draw an eye on the left side of the face using the oval tool. Duplicate the eye and move it to the right of the first eye. Align the eyes so that they align vertically to the top each other (see tip in figure).
    f. Add arms and hands to the snowman using the line tool.
    g. Add color to your shapes as desired.
3. Print your drawing and/or submit your drawing according to your teacher's instructions for grading purposes.

Google Drive Essentials, George Somers

Lesson GR4: Stacking Order

Whenever objects of your drawing overlap in any way, you need to be able to specify the **stacking order** of the objects. The stacking order determines which objects are on top, which ones are in the middle and which ones are at the bottom of the stack.

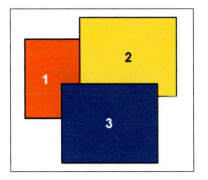

In in the figure to the right, all three boxes are the same size. **Box 1** is on the bottom layer, **Box 2** is in the middle layer, and **Box 3** is on the top of the stack.

You can tell Google Drawings where in the stacking order an object is by using the **Arrange > Order** options shown below:

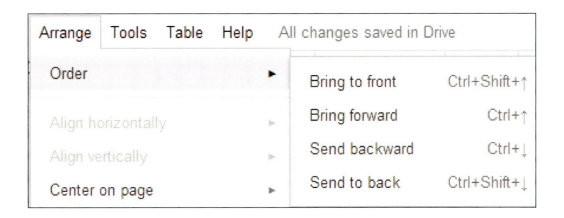

Objects can be brought forward or backward in the stacking order or sent to the back or front of the stack. In this lesson, you'll practice defining the stacking order of the objects in your drawing.

Time to start this lesson's tutorial.

Using the sample as a guide, complete the following tutorial.

1. In Google Drive, create a new drawing document and rename it "Lesson GR4".
2. In separate areas of your drawing area, draw the following shapes: a **3D cube**, **3D cylinder**, a **lightning bolt**, a **circle**, and a **right arrow**.
3. Color your shapes as desired.
4. Position each object on the cube as shown on the sample. Size each object accordingly.
5. For each object on the cube, select the object and use the **Arrange > Order** options to either send the object forward/backward or send it to the back or front of the stacking order so that your drawing matches sample below.

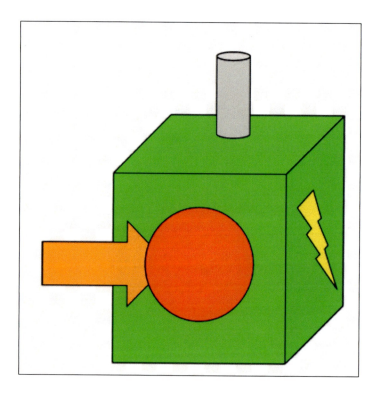

Are you ready for Opportunity GR4? Of course, you are! Let's do it!

Opportunity GR4

Stacking Order

1. Create a new **Google Drawings** document in Google Drive and **rename** it "OPP GR4".
2. Using the **OPP GR4 Sample 1** below, do the following:
    a. Draw a rectangle with these properties:
        i. Use a light fill color.
        ii. Use a border 4px.
        iii. Add centered text with a font of **Arial** size **24**.
        iv. Number your first rectangle "1".
    b. **Duplicate** the rectangle until there are 12 rectangles and arrange them as shown below.
    c. Number the other rectangles 2 through 12 as shown below.
    d. Select each odd-numbered rectangle and shade them with another light color fill. Your odd-numbered rectangles should now be one color and the evens will be another.

OPP GR4 Sample 1

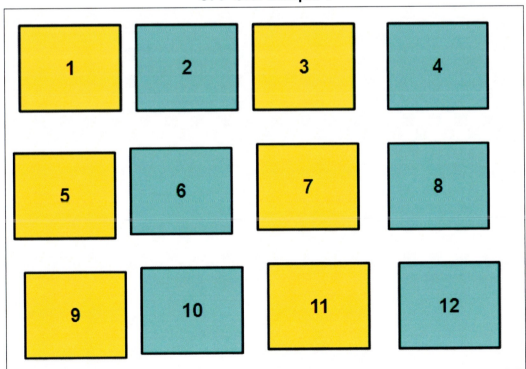

Google Drive Essentials, George Somers

3. Use **Arrange > Order** options to arrange your boxes as shown in **OPP GR4 Sample 2** below. Make sure your stacking order matches the sample.
4. Print your drawing and/or submit your drawing according to your teacher's instructions for grading purposes.

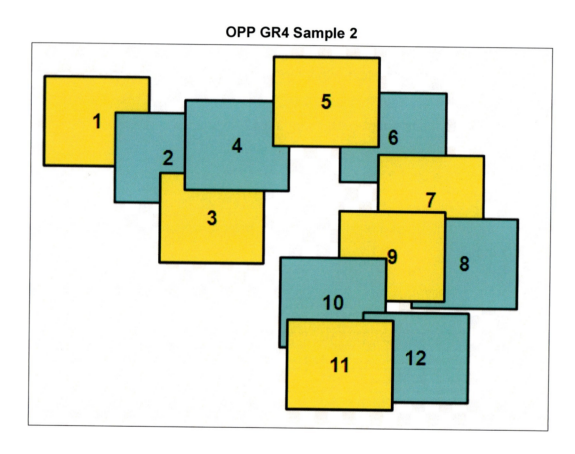

OPP GR4 Sample 2

Made in the USA
Middletown, DE
12 July 2023